"This is a 'must read' for executives and managers at all levels. The ADKAR model clearly explains why change sometimes is very successful and other times fails miserably. This book provides a simple, yet effective model for any change program to follow to minimize implementation risks."

Jeffrey A. Randall, PhD, PMP
CACI International Inc.

"Change is often a complex and difficult process. The ADKAR model makes it something we can all understand, and even enjoy. This book is a valuable resource for business leaders and project managers to effectively apply change management techniques on projects of all sizes and types."

Lori Bocklund
President
Strategic Contact, Inc.

"If you are looking for a change management methodology that is easy to grasp and apply, this book has it. I found the ADKAR model sufficiently robust to be applied in a wide variety of organizational settings. ADKAR is not a buzz word or the latest fad; it is a sure and practical pathway for all organizations implementing change."

Rahul Sur
Management Consulting Officer and Learning Coordinator

"A powerful addition to the change management body of knowledge."

Margaret Poropat
Department of Main Roads, Australia

"The use of strategies and case studies really gives the material credibility. This is more effective than just reading theories. I value the practical application."

Brian Barnes MBA, PMP
Sr. Manager, Software Validation
BIOSITE

"It is easy enough for a novice to follow and comprehensive enough for an expert to appreciate. I've tried the model on both small (controlled) change projects and large-scale, multi-site, organizational-level change projects. The ADKAR model works! This is fool proof. I highly recommend this book and especially this model to everyone."

Rita Wilkins, MSMOB
Planned Care Coordinator
Lake County Health Department and Community Health Center

"A 'new lens' to observe and influence change."

Gary Lyon
Ashland, Inc.

"ADKAR makes change management understandable and useable."

Frank Petrock, Ph.D.
The LEAD Institute/General Systems Consulting

"ADKAR is one of those concepts that will profoundly change the way you interact with others, both personally and professionally. Based on voluminous research, Jeff Hiatt constructed the ADKAR model as a framework for change, and offers simple, yet highly effective, tools and techniques to address the challenges of change."

James J. Schnaible
City of Albuquerque

"Managing change requires new thinking on the part of change managers. New thinking leads to new models for change. New models require organised frameworks and tools to enable the smooth implementation of the desired change. ADKAR has it all."

Dr. Eric Graham
ETAS (WA) PTY LTD
Registered Training Organisation #1967

"I found the book to be an excellent conversation of the personal change approach – a methodological approach to the art of change. It has a balance between methodology and the practical application of change tools for professionals."

Rick Kneebone
Global Change Initiative Manager
Molson Coors Brewing Company

Jeffrey M. Hiatt

ADKAR: a model for change in business, government and our community

Prosci Learning Center Publications
Loveland, Colorado

Printed in the United States of America

Library of Congress Control Number: 2006903241

Hiatt, Jeffrey M.
    ADKAR: a model for change in business, government
    and our community

    p. cm.

    ISBN 978-1-930885-50-9 (paperback)

    ISBN 978-1-930885-51-6 (hardcover)

    1. Organizational change. 2. Change
    management. 3. Leadership. I. Title.

    HD58.8 2006

    658.4'06--dc20

Prosci Research
Loveland, Colorado, USA

The paper used in this publication meets the requirements of the American National Standard for Permanence of Paper for Printed Library Materials Z39.49-1984.

Volume discounts and direct orders are available from Prosci Research by calling 970-203-9332 or by visiting www.change-management.com

To Mary, Paul and Anna

Acknowledgments

When the development of a model and book takes more than 10 years, acknowledging contributors becomes an important yet difficult task. This book could only be written because of the insights, stories and personal testimonials provided by work colleagues, clients and close friends. In no particular order, and with hopes of not leaving someone out along the way, I acknowledge these contributors.

During the eight years of change management research with Prosci that preceded this text, Alice Starzinski, Dave Trimble, Jennifer Brown, Neil Cameron, Jennifer Waymire, Kathryn Love, Adrienne Boyd, Becky Fiscus and Kate Breen collected and analyzed data from hundreds upon hundreds of organizations. Tim Creasey was a thought leader and research champion. Kathy Spencer, James Pyott and Jenny Meadows brought structure and order to the writing. J.J. Johnson was a true storyteller, and Tara Spencer became the model's evangelist. Marisa Pisaneschi and Maggie Trujillo served as our voice to the customer. Kirk Sievert, Gene Sherman and Jim Simpson helped me see new ways to apply the model. Jeanenne LaMarsh provided the spark that made 'managing the people side of change' become a passion for this analytical engineer. Lori Bocklund, James Schnaible, Dr. Phil Harnden and Dr. Frank Petrock went above and beyond with the final manuscript review, providing fundamental ideas for improving the text overall. Herb Burton, a long-time mentor, has always been a wonderful sounding board.

More than 60 individuals participated in the final book review, and I thank each of you for your time and energy.

Jeff

Preface

This preface attempts to answer the questions, "Why should I read this book?" and "What's in it for me?" For business and government leaders managing change, the challenges and demands are non-stop. The stakes are high and so is the stress. We at the Change Management Learning Center deal with benchmarking data from hundreds of organizations and talk with project leaders every week. Many new techniques for managing change result from these interactions. The ADKAR model provides a primary framework to bring together new and traditional methods for managing change and is instrumental in diagnosing failing changes.

For nearly 20 years, both as an engineer with Bell Laboratories and as a project leader for other companies, I worked large-scale process, system and organizational change. My experiences were a mixture of successes and failures. A common theme around project failures was resistance to change; as one of my colleagues joked, "All of our change initiatives would have gone great if it weren't for all the people involved."

The more I immersed myself in the field of change management to address this resistance issue, the more complex the problem became. One would think that engineers are fairly good problem solvers. This solution, however, was proving elusive. After nearly eight years in undergraduate and graduate engineering, I was surprised to find the most challenging problems dealt with people and not with things.

The catalyst for the ADKAR model was a reaction to the myriad of change management approaches that were proposed by management consultants and authors. These approaches focused on many activities to manage change, including assessments, communications, training, coaching and so on. I struggled with the idea that these change management activities were surely not an endpoint by themselves. From a business perspective, I was constantly bothered by the absence of an end result that these activities should produce.

This focus on results turned out to be the genesis for the ADKAR model. I began to ask the question "Why?" every time I heard about another change management tactic or approach. In other words, "Why would you do that?" and "What is your desired outcome?" For example, communications is commonly cited as an essential element for managing change. Why? One objective of communications is to build awareness of the need for change and to share with employees why the change is happening. Employees want to understand the nature of the change and the risks of not changing. This led to the first component of ADKAR: *awareness*.

By examining a large number of change management activities and mapping them into their desired results, I was able to envision a fairly simple model that included five building blocks for change: awareness, desire, knowledge, ability and reinforcement. During the early drafts of the model, some of the words changed. For example, I struggled with the term *desire* versus *motivation*. I settled on *desire* because my research suggested that motivation was only one component that created the desire to change. On first analysis this model met my "engineering" criteria: It was simple and identified the desired outcomes for different change management strategies and tactics.

The Change Management Learning Center began studying ADKAR as a model for change. The more research we did, the more convinced we became that this simple model for managing change was essential in both the learning process for new change leaders and in the effective application of change management activities. We were finding support for ADKAR based on research data from hundreds of project teams. As we began sharing our benchmarking data in reports and publications, we found a growing interest in this model.

Recently we added ADKAR to our change management training programs. Even though we spend just a short time during the three-day program on this model, the most commonly cited highlight of the entire program from the feedback forms is ADKAR. I still ask people in our change management training courses why they gravitate to the ADKAR model, and the answer is almost always the same: "It is results-oriented and easy to apply in a number of change settings."

Over the past several years, ADKAR has become the most sought-after model from the Change Management Learning Center, with adoption by many Fortune 100 companies, the US Department of Defense and other government agencies around the world. Many companies that provide change management training for their managers choose this model as the primary tool for working with employees during change.

I did not then, nor do I now, view this model to be some type of breakthrough, but rather a framework for understanding and applying many approaches for managing change. ADKAR is a perspective on change that enables other change management tactics to have focus and direction. I very much credit those authors and practitioners whose books and real-life experience have influenced my understanding of change management. William Bridges, John Kotter, Daryl Conner, David McClelland, Frank Petrock, Peter Block, Jeanenne LaMarsh, Patrick Dolan, Richard Beckhard and Reuben T. Harris are a few of the writers and practitioners who have shaped my views on this topic.

This book is a formal presentation of the ADKAR model.

In addition to presenting ADKAR, I will also attempt to answer three fundamental questions about change using this model.

- Why do some changes fail when others succeed?

- How can we make sense of the many methods and tactics for managing change?

- How can we lead change successfully, both in our personal lives and professional careers?

The staff of the Change Management Learning Center has contributed many case studies, research findings and perspectives that hopefully will make this book engaging and applicable to both your work and life.

ADKAR: a model for change in business, government and our community

Table of Contents

Chapter 1
ADKAR: Overview

Why do some changes fail while others succeed? After extensive research with hundreds of organizations undergoing major change, I have observed that the root cause of failure is not simply inadequate communications or poor training. Success is not to be found in excellent project management alone, or even the best vision or solution to a problem. The secret to successful change lies beyond the visible and busy activities that surround change. Successful change, at its core, is rooted in something much simpler: How to facilitate change with one person.

The ADKAR model presented in this book is a framework for understanding change at an individual level. This model is then extended to show how businesses, government agencies and communities can increase the likelihood that their changes are implemented successfully.

The ADKAR model has five elements or objectives as shown in Figure 1-1. It is useful to think of these elements as building blocks. All five elements must be in place for a change to be realized.

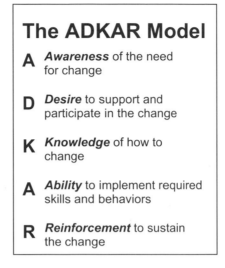

Figure 1-1 The ADKAR Model

Awareness represents a person's understanding of the nature of the change, why the change is being made and the risk of not changing. Awareness also includes information about the internal and external drivers that created the need for change, as well as "what's in it for me."

Desire represents the willingness to support and engage in a change. Desire is ultimately about personal choice, influenced by the nature of the change, by an individual's personal situation, as well as intrinsic motivators that are unique to each person.

Knowledge represents the information, training and education necessary to know how to change. Knowledge includes information about behaviors, processes, tools, systems, skills, job roles and techniques that are needed to implement a change.

Ability represents the realization or execution of the change. Ability is turning knowledge into action. Ability is achieved when a person or group has the demonstrated capability to implement the change at the required performance levels.

Reinforcement represents those internal and external factors that sustain a change. External reinforcements could include recognition, rewards and celebrations that are tied to the realization of the change. Internal reinforcements could be a person's internal satisfaction with his or her achievement or other benefits derived from the change on a personal level.

The elements of the ADKAR model fall into the natural order of how one person experiences change. *Desire* cannot come before *awareness* because it is the awareness of the need for change that stimulates our desire or triggers our resistance to that change. *Knowledge* cannot come before *desire* because we do not seek to know how to do something that we do not want to do. *Ability* cannot come before *knowledge* because we cannot implement what we do not know. *Reinforcement* cannot come before *ability* because we can only recognize and appreciate what has been achieved.

The lifecycle for ADKAR begins after a change has been identified. From this starting point, the model provides a framework and sequence for managing the people side of change. In the workplace, ADKAR provides a solid foundation for change management activities, including readiness assessments, sponsorship, communications, coaching, training, recognition and resistance management.

Chapters 2 through 7 introduce each element of the model with case study examples. Once the foundation for the model is established, Chapters 8 through 14 provide concrete strategies and tactics for achieving each element of the model.

Chapter 2

Awareness

The first step to enable a change is to create *awareness* of the need for change. Awareness is the first element of the ADKAR model and is achieved when a person is aware of and understands the nature of the change, why it is needed and the risks of not changing.

Pineapple growers in Ghana were resistant to implementing codes of practice for their crops. Codes of practice are techniques and methods for growing crops that improve the overall health and safety of the product and associated processes. An awareness campaign was initiated to inform growers that certain countries would not purchase agricultural products without code compliance. In fact, big buyers like UK supermarkets considered code compliance a prerequisite for buying. Farmers in Ghana were also made aware that other farmers were cutting costs through reduced pesticide use by adopting the codes of practice. Because the UK supermarkets were considered the big prize for these farmers, this campaign was effective. Awareness-building focused on profitability and the risk that some markets would be out of reach if a change was not made. Building awareness of the need for change was the first step to enable this change.[1]

Meeting the human need to know "why" is a critical factor in managing change. At the first evidence of change, people begin to seek this information. When change occurs in the workplace, employees will ask their peers, supervisors and friends:

Why is this change necessary?

Why is this change happening now?

What is wrong with what we are doing today?

What will happen if we don't change?

In a 2005 study with 411 companies undergoing major change projects, the number one reason for resistance to change was lack of *awareness* of why the change was being made.[2] Project managers of these major change initiatives stated that employees and managers alike wanted to know the business reasons for the change so they could better understand the change and align themselves with the direction of the organization. When asked what messages were the most important to share with employees, project managers stated:

> *Communicate the business need for change and explain why the change is necessary; provide the compelling reasons for the change and emphasize the risk of not changing.*

Some managers argue, however, that employees do not need to know the reasons behind every change. They hold the position that employees are compensated for performing a job, and if that job should change, employees should just do those new tasks rather than ask *why* a change is needed.

When an organization has a high degree of control over an individual's actions and choices, whether through circumstance or mutual agreement, this viewpoint may not be an obstacle to change. For example, medical first responders and firefighters have established protocols and a clear chain of command. When emergency circumstances dictate a change in their response, rescue personnel do not stop to ask *why*. Likewise, when soldiers are operating under a crisis situation, the long-honored nature of military relationships enables rapid compliance to change. However, these extraordinary, time-critical situations are more the exception than the rule.

In many high-performing workplace environments, an organization's control over an individual's day-to-day work is low. For example, manufacturing employees using Six Sigma techniques are engaged in the everyday improvement of work processes. These employees take ownership of both the work product and associated procedures. They assume accountability for the results of their work. In these circumstances, organizations have a lower degree of direct control over their employees' day-to-day activities. When changes are mandated from above, these employees are the first to ask "Why is this change being made?"

An organization's control over the day-to-day tasks of professional employees is even less. The information age has brought more educated and mobile employees into companies. When they do not understand the reasons for change or do not agree with those reasons, they can create formidable resistance and barriers to change within an organization.

Groups or individuals who attempt to implement change within the general public have the greatest challenge, as these organizations have the least amount of control over their audience. New South Wales State Emergency Service in Australia sought to change the readiness of the public to deal with storm hazards. They wanted to mitigate the effects of disaster, including the loss of life and associated storm costs. Flood and storm costs were exceeding $200 million annually. The State Emergency Service used awareness-building as the first tactic in implementing change. Wide-scale public information channels were used, including brochures, radio advertisements and newspaper interviews. Well-remembered and often tragic disasters were commemorated with special community events to bring awareness to the potential threats. The goal was to create sufficient awareness with the general public that action would be taken on the local level to prepare for disasters. By implementing this change, the loss of life and the costs associated with major floods and storms could be reduced.[3]

Organizations that seek to drive change regarding environmental issues have a similar challenge. City officials in Graz, Austria provide an excellent example of enabling change through awareness-building with an audience over which they have no direct control. The aim of their campaign was to raise awareness about emissions from automobiles in order to promote the purchase of low-emission cars and to encourage alternate transportation methods. The campaign centered on reduced parking tariffs for low-emission automobiles, including hybrid gas/electric cars. The concept was simple: these vehicles would pay less to park. A special parking sticker was issued for low-emission vehicles, making it clear to the general public which cars qualified for this discount. Not only were parking fees lowered for these cars, the vehicles were clearly identified. The net effect was an increase in public awareness about the emissions issue and which cars they could buy to help with this problem.[4]

In a similar effort, the US Environmental Protection Agency has long struggled with the public's disposal of computer equipment. The EPA estimates that about 80 million computers are thrown out annually. The impact on landfills is significant, especially related to PC monitors that contain lead. To bring awareness to this issue and initiate a change toward recycling of computer hardware, the EPA contracted with Dell to lease 100,000 computers over the course of the agreement and to have Dell become the primary provider of recycling services to the EPA. In this role, Dell, a primary manufacturer of PC equipment, will assist the EPA in addressing a major issue facing landfills. A senior manager of Dell's Asset Recovery

Services group stated, "We still have a long journey in terms of creating awareness and sufficient programs to address the recycling issue."[5]

In this example, the EPA leveraged their purchasing power to access a channel of communication to the general public through Dell. With this deal, the EPA is increasing awareness of the impact on landfills of computer hardware and gaining Dell's support in the awareness-building process.

Building awareness of the need for change requires the following components to be addressed:

- What is the nature of the change and how does the change align with the vision for the organization?

- Why is the change being made and what are the risks of not changing?

- How will the change impact our organization or our community?

- What's in it for me (WIIFM)?

Given this straightforward list of topics, is awareness-building just a matter of effective communications? In most cases, the answer is no. Multiple factors, as shown in Figure 2-1, influence how readily people recognize the need for change, including:

Factor 1 – A person's view of the current state

Factor 2 – How a person perceives problems

Factor 3 – The credibility of the sender

Factor 4 – Circulation of misinformation or rumors

Factor 5 – Contestability of the reasons for change

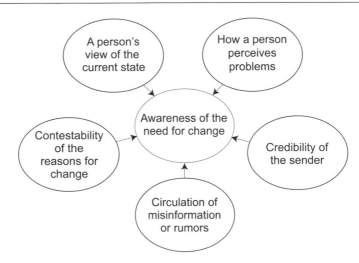

*Figure 2-1 Factors influencing awareness of
the need for change*

Each of these factors directly influences the success of creating awareness of the need for change.

Factor 1 – *A person's view of the current state*

Individuals who strongly favor the current state and who have significant time, energy or money invested in how things are done today may initially *deny* the reasons for change or *discredit* those reasons in favor of maintaining the status quo.

> *If it's not broke, don't fix it.*

> *We have been doing it this way around here ever since
> I joined the company.*

> *What is wrong with what we are doing now?*

On the other hand, people who strongly oppose the current state may seize upon the reasons for change as further evidence for their belief that a change is needed.

I told you that changes were needed a long time ago.

It's about time someone listened to me.

When individuals are dissatisfied with the current state, they may use an awareness message to justify their past position, even if it is not related to the change at hand. How people react to awareness messages, and the amount of resistance they ultimately express, is strongly related to how they feel about their current situation. The more comfortable and invested they are in the current state, the more likely they are to ignore or discredit the reasons for change. The more discontent they are with the current state, the more likely they will listen to and internalize the reasons for change.

Factor 2 – *How a person perceives problems*

This second factor relates to a person's cognitive style and how they internalize new information against the backdrop of their current perceptions. Dr. Michael J. Kirton, in his book <u>Adaption-Innovation</u>, writes about two cognitive styles of business managers on a spectrum of more *adaptive* to more *innovative*.[6] He states:

> *Adaptors more readily anticipate challenges and threats from within the system (often devising, in good time, plans to economise, downsize, etc.), whereas innovators are more ready to anticipate events that might beckon or threaten from outside, such as the early signs of changing tastes and markets or significant advances in technology that have not yet been fully exploited.*

In other words, employees whose style is more *adaptive* are more aware of internal threats. Employees whose style is more *innovative* are more aware of external drivers for change. Kirton goes on to say:

> *In research, it was noted that every manager tended not only to miss some cues that were picked up by others, but also found others' warnings irritating and distracting 'to real issues' (i.e., ones they could see clearly).*

This factor of "style" relates to *how* individuals approach problems and how they internalize and evaluate warnings that change is needed. Each of us has a unique way of processing information and solving problems. We each deal with things in our own way and in our own time. This "style" factor suggests that broad and general communications may not always, by themselves, create awareness of the need for change. For example, awareness messages that focus on threats from *within* the system may miss Kirton's *Innovators,* while messages that focus on *external* cues may irritate Kirton's *Adaptors.*

Factor 3 – *Credibility of the sender*

The credibility of the sender of awareness messages directly impacts how an individual will internalize that information. Depending on the level of trust and respect for the sender, recipients of the message will view the sender either as a credible source or someone not to be believed.

In the workplace, employees have specific expectations related to communications surrounding change. Messages about *why* the change is being made and how the change aligns with the business strategy are expected from the person near or at the top of the organization. Messages about *how* the change will impact employees locally and how the change may impact them personally are expected from their immediate supervisor.[7]

People also weigh the message against the backdrop of the organization's track record with change. If the organization has a history of false alarms or failed changes, individuals will tend to disregard new information even if it represents a true threat. For example, communities that face frequent storm hazards like those cited in the New South Wales case study may not heed awareness messages if the previous two or three warnings turned out to be false alarms.

Regardless of the real nature of the reasons for change, these perceptions of the messenger's credibility can greatly influence a person's willingness to acknowledge the awareness message. In some cases individuals will simply not believe the reasons for change or will not take them seriously.

Factor 4 – *Circulation of misinformation or rumors*

This fourth factor relates to the presence or absence of distorted or incorrect information in the background conversation. For example, if business managers have withheld information from employees about the change, and rumors have spread among employees, these rumors may have clouded the facts and have created barriers to building awareness. Employees may have trouble sorting out real information from fabricated or distorted information, and they may be more likely to listen to rumors than to their own manager. Supervisors may spend more time correcting misinformation than they would have spent communicating the right information in the first place.

Factor 5 – *Contestability of the reasons for change*

The final factor that can impact awareness-building is the contestability of the reasons for change. Some changes will have external and observable reasons that are difficult to dispute. These conditions are more often present in changes that are a reaction to an external event or trend, or are driven by forces outside of the organization.

For example, changes that are made within a nuclear energy plant to comply with new waste disposal regulations have external drivers for the change. The reason *why* the change is needed is compliance with a new law. The *risk* of not changing includes fees or penalties. Another example would be a company that is changing their product or service offering in response to dropping market share and declining revenues. The reasons for change are external (marketplace-driven) and are observable. The risk of not changing is potential downsizing, lost opportunities or perhaps bankruptcy.

The presence of external drivers is not always sufficient, as evidenced by the controversy surrounding the Kyoto Protocol to reduce greenhouse gas emissions. Visible evidence such as glacier recession and increases in ocean surface temperature stirred the debate over the effect of human activity on global climate. Arguments arose about whether or not these climate trends are caused by industrial activity or by natural, long-term climate cycles. In other words, a person or group that opposed this treaty could contest the reasons for the change based on a myriad of scientific data from one side or the other. On the matter of the Kyoto treaty, the position of the United States administration in the late 1990s was to question the degree to which greenhouse gases impacted large-scale climate change. In this example, awareness was affected by the contestability of the reasons for change.

Now consider changes in which the reasons for change are internally oriented without any external drivers. For example, a large utility company proposed rotating senior executives among job functions. The vice president of customer service would become the vice president of sales, the vice president of sales would become the vice president of HR, and so forth. The reasons stated for *why* the change was being made included bringing new leadership styles to each group, increasing the synergy between groups and professional development for the executives. Note that on first review the reasons cited for this change are valid. Also note that they are not driven by external and observable forces. The net result is that a reasonable person may debate the grounds for the change. One vice president may take the position that her leadership style has been effective and that the business results are the best ever for her division. Another executive may argue that he has been sponsoring a major change in his area and that this rotation would be disruptive to the success of that initiative.

This issue of contestability can create a barrier to change. If the reasons for change are debatable, then the time required to build awareness is longer. In some cases, individuals may not accept the reasons for change as valid.

Summary

The first step to enable change is to create *awareness* of the need for change. The following factors influence the process of building awareness within individuals during a change:

- Acceptance of awareness messages is greatly influenced by a person's view of the current state. Those strongly invested in the current state may discredit or deny the reasons for change.

- An individual's cognitive style impacts how they perceive the need for change and how they solve problems; some may already see the need for change, whereas others may be caught off-guard.

- The credibility of the sender of awareness messages and the organization's history with change will weigh heavily on whether or not the awareness message is believed and accepted.

- The presence of misinformation or propaganda in the background conversation can stall efforts to create awareness of the need for change; in some cases, overcoming misinformation presents a major barrier for change.

- Awareness of the need for change is easier to create in the presence of external and observable drivers. Changes driven by internal drivers or by reasons that are debatable face greater challenges to building awareness.

Awareness is the first objective of the ADKAR model. Awareness-building establishes the groundwork upon which individuals can make personal choices about change. What about *desire* to engage in a change? Is having awareness of the need for change sufficient to create desire?

Chapter 3
Desire

*D*esire is the second element of the ADKAR model and represents the motivation and ultimate choice to support and participate in a change. Creating desire poses a challenge, in part because of the limited control we have over another person's choices. Unlike awareness-building, where we can take definitive steps to generate awareness of the need for change, creating the desire to change remains elusive and, by definition, not under our direct control.

For example, the pineapple growers in Ghana could not be forced to follow the codes of practice, but they could be made aware of the potential consequences and benefits so that they could make the best business decision. People may be aware that certain vehicles produce lower emissions through Graz's reduced parking fees campaign, but that does not mean they are going to rush out to purchase a new hybrid car. I may be aware that my PC monitor contains some lead, based on the EPA's program with Dell, but I may not be willing to recycle my computer. Awareness enables people to begin the process of evaluating a change, but does not necessarily result in a desire to change.

Likewise, in the workplace, managers can develop new processes, tools and organizational structures. They can purchase new technology and promote new values for their organization. However, they cannot force their employees to support and engage in these changes.

A common mistake made by many business leaders is to assume that by building *awareness* of the need for change they have also created *desire*. Resistance to change from employees takes them by surprise and they find themselves unprepared to manage this resistance. Understanding the underlying factors that influence an individual's desire to change is an important first step to achieving this element of the ADKAR model. Four factors, as shown in Figure 3-1, contribute to an individual's or group's desire to change:

Factor 1 – The nature of the change (what the change is and how it will impact them)

Factor 2 – The *organizational or environmental context* for the change (their perception of the organization)

Factor 3 – An individual's *personal situation*

Factor 4 – What *motivates them* (those intrinsic motivators that are unique to an individual)

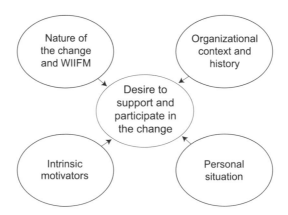

Figure 3-1 Factors influencing desire to support and participate in the change

Factor 1 – *The nature of the change and WIIFM*

A person or group assesses the *nature of a change* on a variety of levels that include "What is the change?" and "How will the change impact me?" This is often termed "What's in it for me?" or WIIFM. They will determine if the change represents an opportunity or a threat. They may also assess how fairly they think the change will be deployed with other individuals or groups. If individuals perceive inequity between groups, this alone can provide an excuse to resist change.

Recall the example of the Kyoto accord. In 2005, nearly seven years after the treaty was ratified, the US administration remained opposed to this agreement. However, the statements for opposing the agreement had shifted focus. In terms of WIIFM, the US administration cited negative impacts on the US economy as the main reason for not joining the accord. They also cited the inequity of the accord in terms of exemptions provided for large contributors of greenhouse gases, including India and China. Note that these statements of opposition in 2005 are rooted in *desire*. This represents a change from the mid 1990s when the discussion centered on *awareness* of the need for change and the validity of those reasons.

Factor 2 – *Organizational or environmental context*

Organizational or environmental context represents how a person or group views the environment that is subject to the change. Because each person's experience is unique, this assessment of the surroundings will vary from person to person. In the workplace, this organizational context includes the success of past changes, how much change is already going on, reinforcements or rewards that were part of past change, the organization's culture and the overall direction of the organization. The implications of these forces should not be overlooked or underestimated, as an organization's history and culture will play a key role in building desire to support a change. For example, if a company has a history of starting changes and not following through, or if they have a track record of allowing some groups to opt out of a change, then these precedents weigh heavily on the willingness of employees to engage in new changes.

Factor 3 – *An individual's personal situation*

Individual or personal context is the third factor that contributes to a person's desire to change. Personal context includes all aspects of a person's life situation, including family status, mobility (are they in a position to be flexible in terms of where they live?), financial security, age, health, career aspirations (are they where they expected to be at this point in their career?), relationships at home and at work, educational background, upcoming personal events and past success in this work environment (promotions, recognition, compensation).

An individual's personal situation plays a large role in their decision-making process related to change. For example, a person's financial situation or health may cause them to make choices related to a change that on the surface do not appear logical, but when understood make perfect sense. Similarly, a change in a person's relationship with a spouse or significant other can cause a fundamental shift in what is important to that person. Each person has a unique capacity to change.

Factor 4 – *Intrinsic motivation*

Intrinsic or personal motivation is the fourth element that contributes to a person's desire to change. Personal motivators are those inherent attributes that make us individuals. They range from the desire to help others and make a difference in our world, to the avoidance of pain or negative consequences. Some of us seek advancement while others want depth in relationships. Some desire respect, power or position. Some strive for financial security. What drives each of us to change is unique and falls along a broad spectrum of motivators.

Personal motivation not only includes what we value, but also our internal belief that we could achieve what we want should we choose to move forward. It is our internal compass that communicates to us the likelihood or probability that we would obtain the desired result from this change.[1]

Lance Armstrong's decision to attempt a 7th Tour de France victory illustrates each of these components that contribute to desire. First, the *nature of the race* was a substantial factor in this decision. The course, the competitors and the prestige of the event were all part of the nature of the race. The visibility and ultimate reward of winning this event played heavily into "what's in it for me." The *environmental context* included his own history with this event, his personal success with previous races, the push from sponsors and the will of his fans to see him win again. From a *personal context*, he had to consider his age, physical conditioning, current family status and other goals that influence such a decision. From the perspective of *personal motivation*, he had to assess what was important to him at that point in his life and the likelihood that he could be successful in the event. The intrinsic motivators had to be sufficient to overcome the daunting challenge of not just participating but also preparing physically for the race.

Summary

Desire is the second element of the ADKAR model. Our desire to support and participate in a change is based on a number of considerations:

- The nature of the change and what's in it for us as individuals

- How we perceive the organization and our surroundings that are undergoing change

- Our personal situation

- What motivates us as people, including our expectation that we could be successful and realize the change

A combination of these factors will ultimately contribute to the behaviors we express when confronted with change.

Once a person has the *desire* to support and participate in a change, the next element in the ADKAR model is *knowledge* of how to change. The question to examine at this point is "If I understand the need for change and I am willing to change, can I reasonably expect that the change will happen?"

Chapter 4

Knowledge

*K*nowledge is the third element of the ADKAR model and represents *how* to implement a change. Knowledge includes:

- Training and education on the skills and behaviors needed to change

- Detailed information on how to use new processes, systems and tools

- Understanding of the new roles and responsibilities associated with the change

When a person has the *awareness* of the need for change and the *desire* to participate and support a change, *knowledge* is the next building block for realizing that change.

"Green" Hotels Association introduced a change in 1993 that has spread throughout hotels in the United States and impacts many business and vacation travelers. After a trip to Germany, Patricia Griffin, founder and president of "Green" Hotels Association, returned with an idea to change the way hotel guests treated bath towels. On the surface this could appear to be a daunting challenge. How could one person initiate a change that would impact thousands of hotel guests? It began with the printing of a small card that would hang on the towel rack in hotel guest rooms. The card, which you may have seen while traveling on business or vacation, essentially says:

Each day we use millions of gallons of water and tons of detergent in hotels to wash guest towels that have been used only once.

Decide for yourself. A towel on the rack means: "I will use it again."

A towel on the floor or the tub means: "Please exchange."

By 2005, "Green" Hotels Association's guest cards could be seen in more than 150,000 guest rooms. Hotels are reporting significant savings in water, utility and detergent costs. This change has helped conserve water and reduce operating expenses while protecting our environment.

Fifteen years earlier most hotel guests would have scoffed at the suggestion that towels be reused. Many people would consider this nothing more than a cost-savings attempt by a "cheap" hotel manager. Imagine the reaction of hotel guests to a sign that reads, *"Please reuse your towel. It saves us money."* Yet, in this case, "Green" Hotels Association was able to successfully implement this change, and nearly every major hotel chain now uses similar towel cards in their guest rooms. What was different about how this change was managed that made it a success?

If you analyze the simple text on this card, notice that *awareness* is the starting point. Many hotel guests may have never considered the implications associated with the simple process of washing towels. Decades of washing every towel and sheet in guest rooms have made us insensitive or perhaps unconscious of the impact this has on the environment.

The card then states clearly: "Decide for yourself." This

simple expression captures the essence of *desire*. It is ultimately up to each hotel guest to participate or not participate in the program.

Finally, the card states how to change: "Hanging up the towel means I'll use it again" and "A towel on the floor means please exchange." This phrase captures the how or the *knowledge* component of the change in very simple terms. Within this simple card the first three elements of the ADKAR model are realized. Since the fourth phase, *ability*, is the simple act of placing towels back on the towel bar, the change took hold. The *reinforcement* for sustaining the change comes from two sources; first the hotel guests' gratification that they have helped in a small way with a large environmental issue, and second, the hotel's expense reduction from using less water, electricity and detergent.

In many cases the required knowledge for implementing a change is clear. For example, if I wanted to realize a life-long dream of sailing, then the required knowledge includes both seamanship and the mechanics of operating a sailboat. I would need to understand how the wind and sails interact to allow the vessel to sail with the wind and to tack into the wind. I would need to understand mariner regulations, safety and navigation.

Many work changes also have straightforward knowledge requirements. For example, organizations implementing large-scale ERP (Enterprise Resource Planning) systems for their order fulfillment and supply chain processes have three primary knowledge challenges: how to use and maintain the system, how the processes will change and how to prepare for the new job roles associated with the work processes.

Other changes, however, do not have such clear-cut knowledge requirements. A network equipment manufacturer implemented a change in their sales force that required their salespeople to move away from selling hardware and to move toward selling customer solutions. The primary selling strategy in this case was to sell based on business value to the client. This strategy was fundamentally different than the traditional model of selling based on the price and features of their equipment.

The compelling need to change was evident in the dropping market share of this long-time market leader. *Awareness* of the need for change came not only from senior business leaders, but was readily visible to the salespeople in declining revenues and dropping stock prices. The salespeople also knew that their future commissions were tied directly to customer purchases. They had a strong *desire* to move away from the old way of selling which was proving ineffective.

The *knowledge* of how to implement this change, however, was not as clear. It could not be distilled down to a simple process change or learning a new system. These salespeople were accustomed to selling products much like a car salesman would sell an automobile; namely, demonstrate the features and capabilities, and then work the price until the customer buys. Shifting to a customer-centric approach based on business value required a completely new way of approaching the sale – a transformation in thinking.

A program was created for these account executives that shifted their orientation away from the products and features of their equipment toward the needs of and value for the customer. This shift in thinking was initially created by having the salespeople learn about the companies they supported. This process included understanding their customers' business operations and financial objectives. The knowledge gap that appeared quickly was that many salespeople did not understand basic financial terminology. After crossing that hurdle, they would spend time analyzing the strengths, weaknesses, opportunities and threats facing that client. A value-based solution would then be created that met the client's needs. The final step was to create a business case to show the costs, benefits and return on investment. This need for a business case presented yet another challenge. Many of the salespeople did not have training in general business management nor did they have MBAs as part of their education. Many had never written a business case.

The process described in this case study is commonly referred to as solution-based selling and is prevalent in many organizations today. The knowledge gap uncovered for these salespeople was profound and created a barrier to change. Some salespeople never gained the necessary knowledge to succeed at this transformation, and a significant fraction of account executives left the company during this transition.

Several factors, as shown in Figure 4-1, will impact the successful achievement of the *knowledge* element of the ADKAR model.

Factor 1 – The current knowledge base of an individual

Factor 2 – The capacity or capability of this person to gain additional knowledge

Factor 3 – The resources available for education and training

Factor 4 – The access to, or existence of, the required knowledge

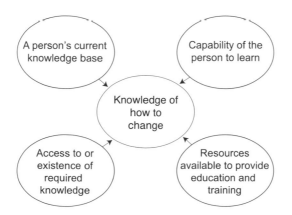

Figure 4-1 Factors influencing knowledge on how to change

Factor 1 – *A person's current knowledge base*

For some changes, a person may already have the required knowledge. In other cases, as with the salespeople in the computer manufacturing case study, the knowledge gaps can be large. The gap between a person's current knowledge level and the knowledge requirement associated with the change will directly impact the probability of success for those individuals. The current knowledge base of an individual could be in the form of education or work experience.

Factor 2 – *Capability of the person to learn*

In addition to the knowledge gap that may exist, each of us has a different capacity to learn. Some people pick up new information easily, whereas others struggle to learn new processes or tools. For example, some people learn new concepts quickly, but have difficulty learning technical skills. For other people, learning new information that requires memorization may be a challenge. In the same way we observe learning differences in our school systems among students, you can expect to see similar differences with adults during the learning process.

Factor 3 – *Resources available to provide education and training*

The third factor that influences *knowledge* is the resources available to provide education and training. In the workplace, this capacity varies greatly from one organization to another. Some companies have extensive resources and funding to deliver training. Other firms struggle to provide any type of structured education to support a change. Resources could include the availability of subject matter experts, instructors, classroom facilities, books and materials, equipment and systems for student use, and funding to support the training program overall.

Factor 4 – *The access to, or existence of, the required knowledge*

For some desired changes, the knowledge may not be accessible or may not exist. Depending on an organization's geographic location, the ready access to knowledge may be a barrier to learning. Some parts of the world have very little access to educational institutions and subject matter experts. Organizations that do not have Internet connectivity also have limitations in terms of their access to knowledge. For other types of changes, the knowledge may not exist, or may not be fully developed. For example, changes that are desired in areas that require engineering or technical knowledge may not be possible because the information is not yet available. Advances in medicine, engineering and other scientific fields occur daily. These advances are often enablers of change when they are developed.

Summary

A combination of factors ultimately determines the degree to which individuals can acquire the necessary knowledge of how to change. These factors include:

- Our current knowledge level

- Our capacity to learn

- The availability of resources

- The access to needed information

Knowledge is the third element in the ADKAR model and is an essential outcome for a change to be realized, both for the individual and for the organization as a whole. Understanding *how* to change can be a simple process in some cases and a transformation in thinking in others.

Does *knowledge* automatically lead to *ability*? This assumption is often made by business managers who use training programs as their primary change management tool. Knowing how to do something and being able to do something is not necessarily the same thing. Under what circumstances does knowledge automatically transfer to ability, as it did with the "Green" Hotels Association case study?

Chapter 5
Ability

*A*bility is the fourth element of the ADKAR model and represents the demonstrated capability to implement the change and achieve the desired performance level.

The presence of knowledge is often insufficient by itself. Someone who recently completed lessons with a golf pro does not walk onto the course and par every hole. Likewise, employees who have knowledge about changes in processes, systems and job roles do not demonstrate immediate proficiency in these areas. Some employees, depending on the change, may never develop the required abilities.

Consider the salespeople in the network equipment company case study from the previous chapter. In this example, all salespeople were required to attend a training program that would fundamentally change how they interacted with their customers. Did it work for all salespeople? No. In fact, about one-third of the participants in the training program expressed reluctance about using this approach before they even returned to work. Another third were optimistic, but uncertain if they could really make it happen. The final one-third left confident and ready. Within 90 days, about 20% of the salespeople were able to implement the new program or some part of the process and tools. This latter group of account executives closed nearly all of the incremental sales using this new approach.

Awareness, desire and knowledge are all essential building blocks, but fall short of realizing change if *ability* is absent. Ability is the demonstrated achievement of the change. Ability is the act of doing, such that the desired objectives of the change are realized. When a person achieves this element of the ADKAR model, the change is visible in action or measurable in terms of effect.

Several factors, as shown in Figure 5-1, can impact a person's ability to implement change, including:

Factor 1 – Psychological blocks

Factor 2 – Physical abilities

Factor 3 – Intellectual capability

Factor 4 – The time available to develop the needed skills

Factor 5 – The availability of resources to support the development of new abilities

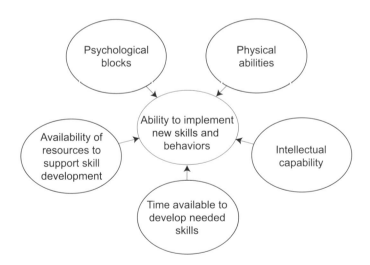

Figure 5-1 Factors influencing ability to implement a change

Factor 1 – *Psychological blocks*

Psychological barriers to change are complex issues that we can recognize as real in terms of their effect, but that we are not always sure how to handle. A close associate (we will call him John for the purposes of this story) wanted to become a volunteer firefighter for his town. He was aware of the need for additional assistance at the fire department from stories in the local newspaper. Being a fireman was appealing to John and he had a strong desire to provide some type of community service, so he joined.

The initial months of the volunteer program were training-intensive. For this town, each firefighter was required to have emergency medical technician (EMT) certification. John passed the course with flying colors. He had always been good in school and this program was no different. John had met three of the requirements for realizing this change. He had *awareness* of the need, a *desire* to serve, and *knowledge* from his new training program.

On John's first emergency call he was summoned to a serious motor vehicle accident. He quickly prepared his gear and uniform, and drove to the accident site. Upon arrival he was confronted with people moving in every direction, but the busy nature of the scene was not what caught John's attention. It was a woman seriously hurt and bleeding on the street. John froze. He could only stand and watch as another paramedic attended to the injured woman. For the first time John felt helpless and unable to act. The sight of blood triggered something for John and he was not able to serve as he anticipated; a week later John left the volunteer fire department. He realized that a majority of their emergency calls were medical in nature. This psychological block was paralyzing for him and prevented him from providing the needed medical care quickly and efficiently.

In the workplace, psychological barriers exist as well. Public speaking, for example, is a fear shared by many. This manifests itself for some employees when participating in large meetings or giving presentations. Some employees do not perform well in these circumstances and later they reflect their frustration at how this nervousness prevents them from demonstrating their real potential.

Factor 2 – *Physical abilities*

For some people, physical limitations may prevent them from implementing change. Take the simple task of keyboarding. Individuals with limited dexterity or arthritis cannot type without tremendous effort. Even when successful, the rate of text entry is very slow. Depending on the performance level required by the change, the new level of performance may simply be outside of the physical abilities of an individual. Sports certainly demonstrate that each of us have limits to our performance. Some of us play sports for fun. Others may have played in high school. Some went on to play in college. A few may play professionally. It is not the absence of knowledge that prevents us from playing sports at higher levels, but rather the absence of ability. We know this to be true by simply observing that some of the best coaches at all levels were not necessarily the best players themselves. Vince Lombardi, for example, is considered one of the greatest coaches in American football. Yet, he never played football in the NFL. In the workplace, physical limitations could include strength, physical agility, manual dexterity, physical size and hand-eye coordination.

Factor 3 – *Intellectual capability*

Intellectual capability can also play a role in developing new abilities. All individuals possess unique skills that fall on spectrums of intellectual ability. For example, some people have a natural talent when it comes to finance and math, whereas others excel at innovation and creativity. Some people are naturally good writers, whereas others struggle to put their thoughts and ideas into words. Depending on the nature of the change, some individuals may have mental barriers to implementing the change. In the case study of the network equipment manufacturer where only 20% of the salespeople were able to change their selling approach, analytical skills became a barrier to change. Many could not develop the abilities around problem solving, financial analysis and business case development within a reasonable time to produce revenue results.

Factor 4 – *The time available to develop the needed skills*

Time can be a factor for many types of change. If a person cannot develop the required skills in the needed time frame, then the change could fail, even if the person might have the potential to develop these abilities given more time. In a business situation, the time frame for implementing change is often driven by external factors outside of the control of managers and supervisors.

Factor 5 – *The availability of resources*

The availability of resources to support a person during this developmental period will also play a role. Resources could include:

- Financial support

- Proper tools and materials

- Personal coaching

- Access to mentors and subject matter experts

The process of developing new skills and abilities is enhanced by the presence of a support structure for an individual. This support structure promotes the cultivation of new skills, but it also can address any knowledge gaps that may be revealed once the change is underway.

Summary

All of these factors – psychological blocks, physical abilities, intellectual capability, time and resources – contribute to our potential to develop new abilities. By definition, *ability* in the context of the ADKAR model is achieved when a person or organization can implement the change and achieve the desired performance level associated with that change.

Ability is the fourth element of the ADKAR model. Once a person demonstrates the desired skills and behavior for the change, has the change process been completed? If individuals have the ability to implement the change, then, as change leaders and managers, are we finished managing this change?

Chapter 6
Reinforcement

*R*einforcement is the final element of the ADKAR model. Reinforcement includes any action or event that strengthens and reinforces the change with an individual or an organization. Examples include private or public recognition, rewards, group celebrations or even something as simple as a personal acknowledgment of progress.

Reinforcement does not always require major events. In a study of customer service employees, the number one recognition desired by customer service agents was a personal thank you and an expression of appreciation by their supervisor. This gesture is meaningful because of the unique nature of the employee-supervisor relationship. It tells employees that they matter and that their contributions are being noticed and valued.[1] Several factors, as shown in Figure 6-1, contribute to the effectiveness of reinforcements, including:

Factor 1 – The degree to which the reinforcement is meaningful to the person impacted by the change

Factor 2 – The association of the reinforcement with actual demonstrated progress or accomplishment

Factor 3 – The absence of negative consequences

Factor 4 – Accountability systems to reinforce the change

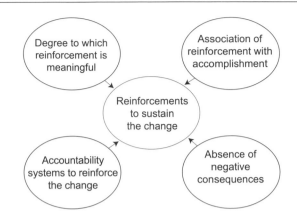

Figure 6-1 Factors that influence reinforcement to sustain change

Factor 1 – *Meaningful reinforcements*

In general, change is reinforced when recognition and rewards are meaningful to an individual. Meaningful from an individual perspective would include several attributes of the recognition:

- The recognition or reward applies to the person being recognized

- The person providing the recognition or reward is someone the individual respects

- The reward is relevant or valuable to the person being recognized

Factor 2 – *Association of the reinforcement with accomplishment*

Most of the time individuals already know when they have succeeded at a change. Recognition simply lets them know that others still care and that the change is important. On the other hand, you probably have experienced a friend or co-worker who struggled to make a change happen, only to find out that no one noticed. In this case, the absence of reinforcement becomes a barrier to sustaining the change.

In the workplace, many project teams ignore the potential of celebrating small successes. When changes are new and when the difficulties of changing are the greatest, opportunities present themselves for celebration. These moments can be turning points for the change. Identifying and acting on these opportunities is a critical part of reinforcing the change.

The converse is also true. If no accomplishment has been made, any attempt at rewards or recognition can backfire. Individuals want to be acknowledged for meaningful contributions and progress. Using recognitions or rewards in the absence of demonstrated achievement reduces the value of the recognition now and in the future.

Factor 3 – *Absence of negative consequences*

When a person experiences a negative consequence for exhibiting the desired behavior, the change process is impeded. Peer pressure is a good example. In the work setting, this can occur if some employees insist on doing things the old way and apply social pressure to their co-workers to do the same. In high schools we observe many types of peer pressure, some good and some bad. If peer pressure is opposing the change, the resulting negative consequence becomes a barrier to the change.

Factor 4 – *Accountability systems*

Accountability for continued performance is one of the strongest forms of reinforcement. For example, individuals who have initiated a fitness program to address health issues are much more likely to sustain the change if they have some type of accountability mechanism. For some individuals, this is a personal trainer who monitors and measures their progress. For other individuals, this could be a friend or workout partner.

For more serious health issues, the accountability mechanism may be frequent checkups with a health care provider.

In the workplace, accountability systems are often tied to job performance and measurements. Once an accountability and performance measurement system is in place, the results of the change become visible on an ongoing basis. When recognition or rewards accompany the achievement of goals or objectives, the probability that the change will be sustained increases.

The greatest risk associated with a lack of reinforcement is a person or group that reverts to old behaviors. Without reinforcement, a person or group may perceive that the effort expended during the transition was not valued. They may seek out ways to avoid the change, and their desire to change will diminish. When NASA returned the space shuttle Discovery safely to earth following the tragedy of the shuttle Columbia, NASA as a whole was recognized for the changes they made to the space program. These changes included efforts to address the culture and values that may have contributed to flawed decision-making, as well as a redesign of major components of the entire system. Yet, even with this recognition for their success, the individual employees at NASA can sustain the change only if they are recognized and their contribution is acknowledged and appreciated.

In the absence of continual reinforcement, it is possible that old habits and norms will creep back into the work environment. If this occurs, then the organization builds a negative history related to change. When the next change comes along, individuals remember how previous changes were managed and how they were treated during the process. The hotel towel reuse case study is another example where reinforcement plays a critical role for hotel guests. If hotel guests support the change and hang their towels back on the rack, but the hotel staff replaces the towels with new ones anyway, then the change is not reinforced. In fact, hotel guests may see this as a reason not to participate in this program going forward.

Summary

Reinforcement is the final element of the ADKAR model and serves three purposes. First, reinforcement sustains the change and prevents individuals from slipping back into old behaviors or old ways of doing work. Second, reinforcement builds momentum during the transition. Finally, reinforcement creates a history that individuals remember when the next change occurs. If change is reinforced and celebrated, then the readiness and capacity for change increases. Reinforcements are successful when:

- They are meaningful to the person recognized.

- They are associated with actual accomplishments.

- There is an absence of negative consequences for desired behavior.

- Accountability mechanisms are in place.

Chapter 7
The ADKAR Model

The ADKAR model has five elements that define the basic building blocks for successful change:

1. Awareness

2. Desire

3. Knowledge

4. Ability

5. Reinforcement

By its nature, ADKAR is an individual change management model. In other words, ADKAR represents the essential elements of change for a single person. When a group of individuals experience change, ADKAR can be used:

- As a coaching tool to support individuals through the change process

- To guide change management activities like communications, sponsorship, coaching and training

- To diagnose a struggling change by performing an ADKAR assessment

In the workplace, missing or weak elements of the ADKAR model can undermine business changes. In the absence of awareness and desire, you can expect more resistance from employees, slower adoption of the change, higher turnover and delays in implementation. If awareness and desire are extremely low, project failure is likely. In the absence of knowledge and ability, you can expect lower utilization throughout the organization, incorrect usage of new processes and tools, a negative impact on customers and a sustained reduction in productivity. In the absence of reinforcement, you can expect individuals to lose interest and revert to old behaviors. Each of these consequences impacts the probability of success for a change and lowers the return on investment (ROI) for the project overall.

When the ADKAR elements are achieved, employees become engaged and energized. The change is adopted faster. Employees contribute ideas and seek out new ways to support the change. Employees have the knowledge and ability to implement the change such that the business goals are realized or exceeded. Employees celebrate success. Flexibility and adaptability become part of the organization's value system; a more change-capable organization results.

Chapters 2 through 6 presented the ADKAR model and identified the factors that influence achievement of each element, as summarized in Figure 7-1. Understanding these factors help change leaders design change management programs that overcome the unique challenges in their organization.

Chapters 8 through 12 present change management tactics and techniques that have the greatest influence on each element of the ADKAR model, including:

- Communications

- Sponsorship

- Coaching

- Resistance management

- Training

ADKAR elements	Factors influencing success
Awareness of the need for change	• a person's view of the current state • how a person perceives problems • credibility of the sender of awareness messages • circulation of misinformation or rumors • contestability of the reasons for change
Desire to support and participate in the change	• the nature of the change (what the change is and how it will impact each person) • the organizational or environmental context for the change (his or her perception of the organization or environment that is subject to change) • each individual's personal situation • what motivates a person (those intrinsic motivators that are unique to an individual)
Knowledge of how to change	• the current knowledge base of an individual • the capability of this person to gain additional knowledge • resources available for education and training • access to or existence of the required knowledge
Ability to implement required skills and behaviors	• psychological blocks • physical abilities • intellectual capability • the time available to develop the needed skills • the availability of resources to support the development of new abilities
Reinforcement to sustain the change	• the degree to which the reinforcement is meaningful and specific to the person impacted by the change • the association of the reinforcement with actual demonstrated progress or accomplishment • the absence of negative consequences • an accountability system that creates an ongoing mechanism to reinforce the change

Figure 7-1 Factors influencing each element of the ADKAR model

45

Each change management activity plays a different role in the change process. For example, communications are instrumental in building awareness of the need for change. Sponsorship is a primary activity for creating awareness, desire and reinforcement. Training plays a key role in developing knowledge and ability (see Figure 7-2).

Change management activities	A	D	K	A	R
Communications	●				
Sponsorship	●	●			●
Coaching	●	●	●	●	●
Resistance management		●			
Training			●	●	

Figure 7-2 Mapping of change management activities to ADKAR

In a similar way, the primary players in the organization contribute differently as well. For example, the primary sponsor (also commonly referred to as the executive sponsor) plays a key role in building awareness and desire, and then provides reinforcement for the change. HR and training, along with the project team, play a primary role in developing knowledge and ability. Managers and supervisors play a critical role throughout the entire process (see Figure 7-3).

Change management players	A	D	K	A	R
Primary sponsor	●	●			●
Leadership coalition	●	●			
Managers and supervisors	●	●	●	●	●
HR and Training			●	●	
Project team			●	●	

Figure 7-3 Mapping of key players during change to ADKAR

Figure 7-4 presents a broader perspective on how change management activities are connected to business results through the ADKAR model. Managing change is not just about the tasks of communications, sponsorship or training. Managing the people side of change is about realizing change faster, with greater engagement (participation levels) and higher proficiency (performance) by all individuals affected by the change. The ultimate goal is to realize the objectives of the change and maximize the total return on investment. These results occur when change management activities create awareness, desire, knowledge and ability to succeed at the change, and when those activities reinforce the change to retain the benefits.

Specifically, Figure 7-4 lists the potential business objectives for a change, including reduced costs, higher revenues, improved quality and return on investment (ROI). Business objectives would also generally include expectations for the project to be "on time and on budget" (see examples in column 4 of Figure 7-4).

Change management strategy development	Change management activities	Change management elements - ADKAR	Business results
Assess the change	Communications	Awareness	On time
Assess the organization	Sponsorship	Desire	On budget
Assess sponsorship	Training	Knowledge	Achieve business objectives
Assess risks and challenges	Coaching	Ability	
	Resistance Management	Reinforcement	- lower costs
Design special tactics			- increased revenue
Form team and sponsor model			- improved quality
Assess team readiness			- return on investment (ROI)

Figure 7-4 – Aligning change management with business results

These business objectives are realized when the organization and individuals have achieved each element of the ADKAR model, including ability (see column 3 of Figure 7-4), since by definition this is the point in which employees have the demonstrated capability to implement the change at the required performance level.

In order to achieve each building block of the ADKAR model, change management activities such as effective communications, active and visible sponsorship, engaged and informed coaching, effective training and carefully directed resistance management must be completed (see column 2 in Figure 7-4).

In order for these *activities* to be successful, a well-defined strategy is needed that includes an assessment of the change and the organization, as well as assessments of the readiness of the project team and sponsors (see column 1). This completes the full cycle linking traditional change management activities to business results through the ADKAR model.

The remainder of this chapter reviews several case studies to examine the application of the ADKAR model to both struggling and successful changes. The case studies selected range from broad and general to narrow and personal to help illustrate the application of the complete ADKAR model.

Hubbert's Peak and Peak Oil Production

On April 20, 2005, Roscoe Bartlett, Representative from Maryland, addressed the US House of Representatives. In this address Mr. Bartlett presented the issues that will face upcoming generations surrounding Hubbert's Peak.[1] Shell Oil scientist M. King Hubbert studied the production and depletion of oil fields in the 1940s and 1950s. He observed that each oil field's production capability followed a bell curve in which the total oil produced from that field increased until it reached its peak, and then gradually declined until the field was exhausted of oil. By taking a view of all oil fields in the United States, he was able to predict in 1956 that US oil production would peak around 1970. This prediction turned out to be accurate, as oil production in the US peaked in the seventies and has declined since then to about one half of peak level. Hubbert made a similar prediction that world oil production would peak in 2000. Since this prediction was made more than 40 years earlier, its accuracy was not as precise as the prediction of the US oil peak. Current geologists predict the peak for world production will occur between 2025 and 2045, with some predicting the peak sooner, depending on total oil consumption rates worldwide.

As world oil production approaches peak capacity, the gap between demand and supply will begin to grow. With the US increasing consumption at a rate of 2% per year and China at 10% per year, the demand for oil continues to rise. When we reach and ultimately "roll over" Hubbert's Peak (visualize a bell curve of which the top is referred to as Hubbert's Peak), the available oil supply flattens and eventually begins to drop off. The growing gap between demand for oil and the dwindling supply of oil over time produces a change in the price per barrel. As the demand and supply gap grows the price per barrel of oil rises.

Because the industrialized world has built an infrastructure based on oil over the past 150 years, this phenomenon will have economic consequences beyond the rising cost of gasoline. Oil has become a fundamental building block in the developed world's infrastructure. Agricultural production, chemicals and plastics, and transportation are three areas that are deeply tied to the availability and price of oil. As the price per barrel of oil increases, so does the cost of goods and services, food and transportation. Because our perception of success equates to increasing productivity and output, we have created an economic model and stock market that is dependent on growth, yet we have built this model on a natural resource that is non-renewable and limited in supply.

During the past 100 years, when we were on the upside of Hubbert's Peak, this was a non-issue as oil production could meet the growth in consumption. As we approach and roll over Hubbert's Peak, consumption growth will rapidly outpace supply availability, and the economic impacts are predicted by some to be substantial.

Many people believe that oil production is not an issue because we have been told that the world's oil supply would not be depleted for several hundred years. What Bartlett, Hubbert and others are trying to communicate is that it is not the ultimate depletion but rather the arrival at peak production that is of concern.

Mr. Bartlett's address to Congress had a central theme beyond creating *awareness* of this issue. He presented data on how rapidly other sources of energy might augment oil. For example, the US government and private industry have been doing research on wind, passive and active solar, geothermal, bio-fuels, nuclear and other energy sources for some time.

Surely we can fill the energy gap. While this ultimately may be true, Mr. Bartlett's message is that the time required to create a sustainable infrastructure based on renewable and other non-renewable energy sources may be longer than we have available. In other words, the window of time in which we could augment oil with other energy sources, including the time necessary to build new infrastructure components, may be too long to avoid catastrophic impacts on our economy. He argues that we need to take immediate action to change both our current consumption rates and our deployment of alternatives in order to ensure that we have the time necessary to implement these alternatives. Bartlett's message is supported by a number of well-respected economists and members of the banking community. An open letter signed by more than 30 prominent business leaders and politicians was sent to the President of the United States in the spring of 2005 urging greater attention to overall risks faced by the dependence on oil.[2] In a separate message, the Federal Reserve System's chairman stated: "Altering the magnitude and manner of energy consumption will significantly affect the path of the global economy over the long term."[3]

If this is such a critical issue, why is change not occurring right now? If our economic future over the next 20 to 40 years is at risk, why aren't we taking action?

Over a six-month period, while leading conference sessions and seminars, I conducted informal assessments of people's awareness of this issue and their perceived need for change. Among more than 800 people at seminars and conferences, less than 10 out of 800 (1.25%) indicated any awareness of this concern. At most seminars with 20 to 50 participants, not a single hand was raised. An AP Wire story was published May 29, 2005, but this article did little to convey the powerful nature of this problem. If you rate awareness of the need for change on a scale of 1 to 5 with "1" being the lowest level of awareness and "5" being the highest, this change rated a "1."

If we apply the same scale to *desire*, then we must look at those factors that create a desire to change. First, the cost per barrel of oil has increased dramatically in the past five years. However, the price of gasoline at the pump has risen only marginally in the US and many people attribute that rise to normal seasonal adjustments and localized events (like what occurred with Hurricane Katrina in 2005). Moreover, the rise has not been enough to make people stop and ask what is happening. In other words, as individuals we are not feeling the pain. Moreover, the time scales for this problem are long and the American public can be slow to react to problems that are not immediate. It cannot be said that there is no desire to conserve, but when assessed across the broad spectrum of industry and public use, the desire to change is low. Since the real impact of this phenomenon may not be felt for 10 to 20 years, there is also no pressing desire to change behaviors today. On a scale of 1 to 5, desire to change at best rates a "2."

For *knowledge*, the overall outlook is quite different. Research into alternative energy sources and methods for conservation have been in place for years. The National Renewable Energy Lab has been operating since 1977 when it started as the Solar Energy Research Institute with work on solar, wind, bio-mass and geothermal energy sources. Other organizations, including the Department of Energy, have been working on nuclear fission, nuclear fusion and hydro-electric sources. The issue with most of these alternatives is that the price per kilowatt produced is usually higher than the cost of energy produced from oil. With nuclear fission and breeder reactors, the waste products are problematic. Nuclear fusion would address most of this issue and produce little waste product, but we are not yet able to sustain a nuclear fusion reaction similar to what powers the sun.

If oil production peaked today, we do not have the infrastructure or capacity to meet the energy demands with alternative sources. In the case of nuclear fusion, this is a knowledge issue. However, with other renewable sources our knowledge level is quite high. On a scale of 1 to 5, this change would rate somewhere between a "3" or "4" depending on how fusion is factored into the assessment.

From the perspective of *ability*, the primary challenge for alternative energy sources is the time required for infrastructure development. As we approach Hubbert's Peak for worldwide oil production, the demand and supply gap may grow faster than we can replace oil with renewable and other non-renewable sources. For example, with a 2% growth rate per year (current US growth rate for oil consumption), the amount of oil consumed is doubling every 35 years. At a 10% growth rate (current Chinese growth rate for oil consumption), the amount of oil consumed is doubling every seven years. You can see that once we approach peak oil production worldwide, the demand pressure will far exceed the available supply. This is what will cause oil prices and gas prices to escalate. In terms of *ability* to implement the change toward alternative energy sources, on a scale of 1 to 5, we rate a low score ("2" or "3") because of the time required to create alternative energy channels and the associated infrastructure compared to the relatively short time window that we may have available.

Over the past 30 years we have had very little *reinforcement* toward a change to alternative sources of energy. For example, individuals who have attempted solar or wind for their homes have struggled to achieve a return on their investment, especially when maintenance costs are included. The housing industry overall has not integrated solar into their building materials or roofing systems, and most single-family homes built today are nearly identical to those built 20 years ago. Alternative sources for transportation have produced little economic reward, and even hydrogen vehicles are not addressing the core issue of energy production. Hydrogen fuel cells are not an energy production source, but rather an energy storage device. Traditional energy sources are still needed to separate hydrogen from water to energize the fuel cell.

If you pull these assessment scores together for Hubbert's Peak and peak oil production, with "1" being the lowest score and "5" being the highest, you have:

- Awareness – 1

- Desire – 2

- Knowledge – 3

- Ability – 2

- Reinforcement – 1

This score can be represented by a simple profile as shown in Figure 7-5.

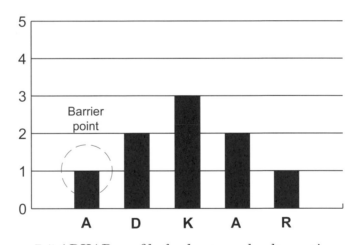

Figure 7-5 ADKAR profile for large-scale alternative energy production

The ADKAR profile for this change is very weak. The barrier point for this change, defined here as the first element that scores a three or lower in the ADKAR assessment, is *awareness*. The complication around this issue is that even if awareness were raised, desire would then become the barrier point. Since our economic models rely on supply and demand to fix the price and therefore curb consumption, desire will not be substantially changed until the price rises considerably. However, by the time the prices rise enough to impact demand, it may be too late to avoid the downturn that will occur within our oil-based economic infrastructure.

The insight provided by the ADKAR model in this case study is that pouring more money into research of alternative energy sources will not by itself create a change to address the issue surrounding peak oil production. Without *awareness* of the need for change and *desire* to engage and participate in the change, implementation of renewable energy sources will stay low, and the risk we face with this issue will remain.

Social Security and Medicare insolvency

Social Security reform in the US has become a major political issue, with the projection that Social Security would become insolvent between 2042 and 2047. Many solutions have been put forth by the Republican and Democratic parties, including progressive indexing, personal accounts, privatization of the Social Security system and changing the payroll ceiling on Social Security and Medicare taxes. So, why do these solutions not move forward? Is it that these ideas are not solid approaches to the problem? If these ideas are not the best ones, can we find other solutions?

This set of questions is a normal response to the Social Security quandary. However, if you look at the needed change through the lens of ADKAR, you will find that the barrier point to change is not about the "right answer."

For Social Security funding changes, the ADKAR assessment profile would look something like:

- Awareness – 5

- Desire – 2

- Knowledge – 3

- Ability – 4

- Reinforcement – 3

The ADKAR profile is shown in Figure 7-6.

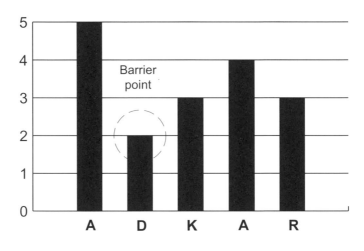

Figure 7-6 ADKAR profile for Social Security reform

A 2005 *USA Today* poll showed that a large majority of Americans are aware of the need for change with Social Security. The widespread media coverage of the issue has raised awareness significantly.

In terms of desire, however, the overall pulse of the nation is quite mixed. By age group, support for Social Security differs dramatically. For example, if you are 50 to 70 years old, you most likely want little or no change to Social Security for fear that your benefits (which you have built over a lifetime) will be reduced. The AARP is also lobbying aggressively for this segment of the population and is appealing directly to the taxpayers through television ads. Essentially the message is "don't do anything dramatic to the US Social Security system."

If you are in the age group 18 to 30, your view may be quite different. Many people in this age group are hearing that it does not matter because Social Security may not be there for them anyway. Taxpayers between the ages 30 to 50 are more prone to support some change, but for many of them the problem is too far out in the future to have an immediate impact.

The net result is that the most impacted group (50-70 years of age), which also is speaking the loudest, has the lowest desire for substantive change to Social Security. Moreover, at this point in history the percentage of taxpayers in this age range is higher than it ever has been in the past. Hence the desire to change is relatively low overall.

Given the political nature of this issue, it will be difficult to move ahead on a solution. In fact, spending more time on how to solve the problem will not be productive until we can increase the overall desire to make a substantial change to Social Security.

Instead, what can happen in these situations is that more time is spent developing a solution that lessens the overall impact on the most outspoken and resistant group. In other words, change is slowed or sub-optimized by a conflict of interests. The final solution is compromised to reduce this resistance. The net result may not be the best overall solution to the insolvency problem, but rather a solution that minimizes the impact on a particular segment of the population.

By using ADKAR as a framework for looking at this change, you can quickly identify the barriers to change and create a more holistic view of what would be required to move this change forward.

Towel reuse program in hotels

The towel reuse program case study that was presented in Chapter 4 is an example of a successful change. The ADKAR profile for this change is:

- Awareness – 5

- Desire – ?

- Knowledge – 5

- Ability – 5

- Reinforcement – 3

The ADKAR profile is shown in Figure 7-7.

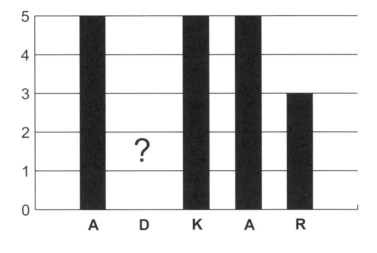

Figure 7-7 ADKAR profile for towel reuse program

Here is an example of a change initiated by a single person that has impacted thousands of hotel guests and has enabled most major hotel chains to adopt a similar program. Why did this change succeed? All of the ADKAR components were high except for desire, and desire is that choice left to the hotel guest. In this case, desire to be environmentally conscious and less wasteful is high for many guests, and hence, the program is successful.

Once you have seen examples of applying ADKAR in different circumstances, you can apply this model to your changes to increase the probability of success. You can also better understand why past changes were successes or failures. For example, why have quality-improvement programs succeeded for some organizations and failed for others? Why has Six Sigma taken off for some companies but struggled in others? Why do technology changes produce significant ROI for some companies and little return for other companies?

Summary

Successful change is realized when two goals are achieved as shown in Figure 7-8 below. First, the business must realize the full implementation of the change so that the business objectives are met. This is the vertical axis of Figure 7-8. Second, the organization must migrate through each element of the ADKAR model so that individuals are able to implement the change and reinforcements are in place to sustain the change. Failure to achieve either goal can result in partially successful or failed changes.

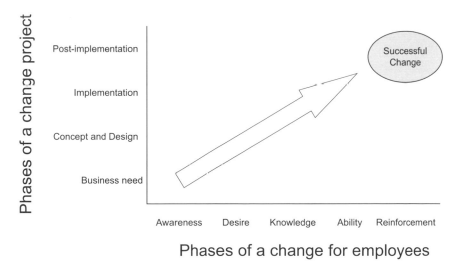

Figure 7-8 Success factors for change using ADKAR

ADKAR is a results-oriented model that provides a framework for how change management tactics and techniques (including communications, sponsorship, readiness assessments, coaching, training and resistance management) come together to produce change. The elements of the ADKAR model must occur in sequence and they are cumulative. In other words, each ADKAR element is a building block. All of the building blocks need to remain present in order for the change to be sustained.

The building block nature of the model is important in terms of application of ADKAR for business, government or community change. The ADKAR elements must be established in order. When an element early in the model is weak, then the change begins to break down. Hence the term "barrier point" is used to refer to the first element of the model that is weak or would be assessed as "low." For example, if both awareness and knowledge were considered low for a specific change, then awareness would be the barrier point for this change and must be addressed before knowledge.

When changes are not succeeding, ADKAR provides a diagnostic framework that is simple and easy to apply. Using this framework you can analyze your change management plan, assess your strengths and weaknesses, and target your energy at the barrier points to change.

For managers and supervisors, ADKAR is an easy-to-learn change management tool that enables them to help employees through the change process.

How can you apply the ADKAR model? Chapters 8 through 13 present how different change management strategies align with and result in movement through each element of the ADKAR model. Chapter 14 presents applications of ADKAR to different situations, including:

- A learning tool for teaching change management, especially when analyzing case studies of successful and failed changes

- A framework for change management teams to evaluate their change management plans

- A coaching tool for managers and supervisors

- An assessment tool for diagnosing changes underway and identifying potential barrier points to change

- A planning tool for behavioral change

Chapter 8

Building Awareness

A common assumption is that awareness building is equal to communications. Yet, sharing information does not always produce awareness. Recall from Chapter 2 the factors that influence the degree to which individuals internalize awareness messages, including:

- Their view of the current state

- How they perceive problems

- The credibility of the sender of awareness messages

- The circulation of misinformation or rumors

- The contestability of the reasons for change

Because of these factors, the act of communicating does not always produce the result of awareness. For example, employees at an energy services company were interviewed after attending a meeting that announced a major restructuring effort. The goal of the meeting was to share the nature of the change and the business reasons for the restructuring. The following quotes from different employees show the range of awareness, from skepticism to total conviction, in the business's reasons for change.

We have heard all of this before. When things are not going well around here, a reorganization is usually the answer.

This is just another attempt to reduce costs.

We are changing so that we can remain competitive and streamline our processes.

Given the current market conditions, we must reexamine how we do business. Our current cost structure is too high and we risk losing business to competitors if some type of action is not taken immediately.

All of these employees were provided the same information. The first employee discredits the information. The last employee demonstrates a strong conviction for the need for change. Because employees internalize information about change in different ways, several observations can be made about the strategy for building awareness. Building awareness is a process; you cannot assume that a single message or event will result in uniform awareness of the need for change. Awareness is not achieved based on the messages sent, but rather how the messages are received and internalized by each person. The only way you can measure awareness is through interactions and feedback. Several change management tactics are effective for building awareness:

Tactic 1 – Effective communications

Tactic 2 – Executive sponsorship

Tactic 3 – Coaching by managers and supervisors

Tactic 4 – Ready access to business information

Before these change management tactics can be applied, it is necessary to brainstorm and discuss the awareness message. The group responsible for developing and implementing the change must have a common understanding of:

- The overall nature of the change and how the change aligns with the vision for the organization

- The reasons this change is necessary or important (why this change is needed now)

- The risk of not changing

- The market changes, competitor threats or customer issues that contribute to the need for change

- When the change needs to be implemented

- Who will be most impacted by the change

Once the foundation for an awareness campaign is established, a combination of change management tactics can be used to create awareness of the need for change.

Tactic 1 – *Effective communications*

Communicating through multiple types of media is the most commonly used method for building awareness of the need for change. Communications could include any of the following channels:

- Face-to-face meetings

- Group meetings

- One-on-one communications

- Email

- Newsletters

- Magazines

- Intranet

- Executive presentations

- Training and workshops

- Project team presentations

- Phone conferences and voice messaging

- Posters and banners

- Memos and letters

- Update bulletins

- Special social events

- Flyers and circulars

- Video conferencing

- Videotapes and plasma screen display boards

- Television

- Radio

- Demonstrations

To support awareness-building, these communication channels should be used only after a communication strategy has been developed. Your strategy should:

1. Identify and segment audience groups.

2. Determine the appropriate messages for each audience.

3. Develop the most effective packaging, timing and channel for these communications.

4. Identify the preferred senders for each audience.

Audience segmentation is essential to ensure that awareness messages are designed specifically for each group. Each group will have a unique context and reference point related to the change. Each group has access to different information on a regular basis and will have different "pain points" and areas of interest. Awareness-building will be most effective when the message is set in the proper context for each audience and the key messages are tailored for each group. Executive managers, for example, already have access to most financial data and changes in the marketplace. Front-line employees, however, may know very little about company finances or changes in the market. To communicate awareness of the need for change, the messages must be meaningful to that audience and must be designed with them in mind.

When developing the most effective packaging, timing and channels for these communications, you should consider:

- What types of communication would be the most effective for each audience group?

- When is the best time to send these messages?

- What communication channels have been the most effective in the past?

Recall from Chapter 2 that the preferred senders of information about change in the workplace include the business leaders of the change and an employee's direct supervisor. Employees want to hear *why* the change is occurring and how that change aligns with the vision for the organization from the business leaders. Employees want to hear *how the change may impact them personally* (what's in it for me) from their direct supervisor. So while general communications will be a critical change management tool, awareness-building requires more than the simple broadcasting of information. Business leaders and managers play an essential role in the awareness-building process.

Tactic 2 – *Executive sponsorship*

The executive sponsor of change is the best spokesperson for communicating *why* a change is needed and the risk of not changing. Employees want to hear from the person in charge, as they believe this person has the broadest perspective and deepest understanding of the state of the business. Business leaders must:

- Share the nature of the change and how that change aligns with the vision for the organization

- Create an understanding of why the change is needed and the risks of not changing

- Establish the priority for the change; the expressed urgency in the message should match the relative importance of the change to the organization

However, a sponsor's role in building awareness goes beyond signing their name to a letter or email, or being the first speaker at events related to the change. Based on research data collected by Prosci in 2005 from 190 project managers,[1] the following roles are the direct responsibility of the primary sponsor:

1. Participate actively and visibly throughout the entire change process; stay engaged with the project team and collect feedback from employees.

2. Build a sponsorship coalition that reinforces the awareness message at all levels; enable peers, direct reports and managers to communicate the reasons for change to employees so that a consistent message is finding its way throughout the organization.

3. Communicate directly with employees; share why the change is happening, the risks of not changing and align the change with the overall direction of the business; repeat these messages through multiple communication channels, including face-to-face interactions.

Tactic 3 - *Coaching by managers and supervisors*

Part of awareness-building for employees is learning what the change will mean for them personally. Awareness of the business reasons for change takes on a unique meaning for each person. Individuals are already aware of their current state: health, comfort level, financial position, relationships, satisfaction with work, family status and the many other factors that comprise their personal situations. When a change is proposed at work, the change is compared with this awareness of self. It is a natural reaction to begin asking *why* as each person begins to map the change against his or her own life. A supervisor is in the best position to help employees understand the reasons for change in meaningful terms and to evaluate how the change will impact each person. Through this process, sponsorship for the change is sustained.

For managers and supervisors to be effective in this role, they must have the opportunity to build awareness of the need for change themselves. Project teams and sponsors of the change must ensure that managers have complete and accurate messages around why the change is needed, the risks of not changing, and what internal and external factors have created a need for change. Managers will also need basic skills and knowledge about change management in order to conduct effective sessions with employees.

Once these preparatory steps are complete, supervisors and managers should discuss the change with their employees. Through face-to-face communications, managers can reinforce the awareness message from the executive sponsor and correct any misunderstandings about the change. They can also collect feedback from employees to better understand the background conversation.

Supervisors and managers should employ both group meetings and one-on-one sessions with their employees. Group meetings are often more convenient and useful for initiating communications. However, group meetings cannot be a substitute for individual discussions about the change. Recall that a key part of awareness-building includes sharing "what's in it for me." These discussions are only effective when you can have candid and confidential conversations with each employee.

This process of meeting with employees as a group and as individuals also helps correct misinformation that may be present in the background conversation. The background conversation surrounding change is powerful and difficult to control. Employees hear business messages and internalize those messages in terms of personal impact. They translate the business change into personal change. The personal impact of the change, along with each employee's point of view, creates the majority of the background conversation. Without supervisors and managers engaging in the process, employees are likely to develop an awareness based on rumors, misunderstandings and inaccurate information. In addition, the project team does not have a reliable channel to collect feedback on where employees stand in the change process without direct supervisor involvement.

Tactic 4 – *Ready access to business information*

Many companies underestimate the power of readily accessible information about company performance, market conditions, environmental factors, competitive threats and changing business priorities. Companies that keep information "close to the vest" with little or no information available to employees face a much greater challenge when building awareness of the need for change.

For example, a software training company used highly trained consultants as subcontractors to teach classes. The training coordinator assigned classes to consultants based on a priority system and how well the consultant matched the client's needs. In some months, the consultants had more work than they could handle. Other months, work was scarce and the consultants expressed concern over the work assignment process. They were frustrated with the unexpected schedule changes that were seemingly shared with them at the last minute. The CEO initiated a change to create better visibility of critical business data for all consultants. This data included training schedules for existing clients, clients in the pipeline, total requests for training information, training revenue and expense data per month. After several months of distributing this data, the tone from consultants changed. Instead of being surprised by changes, they anticipated them. Instead of being frustrated by constant adjustments, the consultants began to suggest ideas to increase business and became engaged in problem-solving. The ready access to information created awareness of the need for change and shifted the role of these consultants from subcontractors to business partners.

Readily accessible information builds awareness on an ongoing basis and supports not just the current change, but changes in the future as well. Creating a communication "culture" that values the sharing of information about the company, the market and the business direction translates directly to increased awareness of the need for change among employees. In some cases, where information-sharing is widespread and commonplace, it is not unusual for employees to be aware of the need for change and to be expecting it.

Frequently asked questions about building awareness

We have had limited success with written forms of communication for building awareness. Why are these communication channels not working?

Over the past eight years in four longitudinal studies by Prosci, project teams report that face-to-face discussions that are honest and straightforward, and that offer details of the change on a personal level, are the most effective form of communication. Face-to-face interactions are more effective than written communications for a number of reasons:

- Not everyone reads every email or newsletter article.

- What the author of an email or document meant as compared with what the reader understood are not always the same. One-way communications do not have the ability to correct these misunderstandings.

- Often emails or articles are not authored by a "preferred sender" – the person that an employee would respect or trust to convey the awareness message.

- The most effective communications include not only content, but also tone and body language. Written information cannot convey these other forms of communication. Often employees will key off the reactions of others around them. Getting those "nods of agreement" in face-to-face interactions can be half the battle.

Our executive sponsors believe they have repeated the message many times and that employees do not want to hear it anymore. What can we do to keep our sponsors engaged in this process?

A rule of thumb is that employees need to hear a message five to seven times before that message is cemented into their thinking. Now multiply that factor by the number of groups throughout an organization. It is easy to understand why an executive may think that a message is being repeated unnecessarily. However, data shows that the most common cause of resistance to change among employees is lack of awareness of why the change is happening. Because executives are commonly involved at the onset of projects, they often communicate the reasons for change very early in the change process. However, employees may not be ready to listen until the change is near implementation (when it begins to impact them personally). Executives may need to see evidence that the awareness message needs to be repeated. You may consider using an ADKAR assessment prior to implementation of the change to measure the level of awareness among different groups in the organization. Then share this data with the executive sponsor to help them target their sponsorship activities.

If we do a good job at building awareness, will this automatically create desire?

It is easy to assume that *your* intrinsic desire to support a change, based solely on awareness, is inherent in other people. In other words, I may think that if awareness caused me to want to change, then it will have the same effect on others. The reality is that desire to engage in a change is based on more than our intrinsic motivators, and even those intrinsic motivators are unique to each person. The nature of the change, my personal situation and the history I have with the organization all play a role in my ultimate desire to support a change. Awareness may create desire in some fraction of the population, but you should not assume that awareness automatically creates desire for everyone.

Is awareness-building focused more on what is changing or why the change is being made?

These two topics are difficult to separate for most changes. Explaining why a change is needed is integral to understanding the nature of the change itself. However, once employees understand the general nature of the change, you should avoid focusing your communications on the details of the solution.

The first question employees have is *why*. The details surrounding the *how* are only of interest when you have awareness of the need for change and a desire to engage in that change. A common mistake I observe with project teams is the strong tendency to create a story around the future state. Since they have invested time and energy in solving the business problems and designing the future state, they have an almost undeniable urge to share their design work. Unfortunately, at the onset of a change, employees want to understand the nature of the change and why the change is happening. Details about the future state often fall on deaf ears as employees struggle to sort out why a change is even necessary. This mistake is a case of jumping right to the *knowledge* stage of the ADKAR model before passing through *awareness* and *desire*. The time will come later when employees will seek knowledge about the details of the future state and how the change will be made.

My sponsor does not believe that he or she needs to have an active and visible role in the change process. Can we build awareness without the sponsor's involvement?

Several factors will influence the success of an awareness-building campaign, not the least of which is the credibility of the sender. Project teams have overwhelmingly reported that active and visible executive sponsorship of the change is the number one success factor for a project overall. Employees have stated that the executive sponsor is the "preferred sender" of messages related to why the change is being made. This data is ignored at peril to the project. Allowing a business leader to delegate their sponsorship will have direct consequences to the project's success. Can you build awareness without his or her involvement? You can certainly make forward progress through many other channels. Can you build sufficient awareness to move the change forward? That depends on the nature and size of your change, and the change-readiness of your organization.

In some cases you may build a limited amount of awareness, but ultimately fail at the *desire* element of the model.

Is it necessary to create a "burning platform" in order to create awareness of the need to change?

A "burning platform" is a term used to describe an extremely urgent or compelling business situation in order to convey, in the strongest terms, the need for change. Using this process, you can get people's attention and build awareness of the need for change very quickly. The only caveat is that not every change can have a burning platform. If this were to become the norm, employees may begin to ignore the message (not everything can be an emergency). As the old story goes, you do not want to be caught "crying wolf" for every change, in case you find yourself really faced by a wolf and no one responds to your call.

What if employees do not believe in or agree with the reasons that are being stated for the need for change?

If a business or organization is making a change, they most often are making the change to respond to a *real* threat or to act on a *real* opportunity. If this is the case, then employees will need an opportunity to understand the reasons for change in more detail. Since employees are not typically exposed to the same information that caused business leaders to initiate a change, this process will take time.

If, on the other hand, the change has been ill-conceived and the reasons for the change are not substantial, it may not be possible to build awareness of the need for change. In these cases the change could fail early in the process or struggle during implementation. If employees do not believe the awareness message because of a history of past failures within the organization or because of poor credibility of the sender, these will be difficult hurdles to overcome. It is sometimes necessary to deal with the organization's history directly or find alternate senders of the awareness message.

It is important to separate a disagreement over the reasons for the change from any debate over the solution or future state. A debate about the solution is very different from a debate over *why* a change is needed. A debate over why a change is needed impacts the ability to create *awareness* of the need for change. A debate over the future state of the change may impact a person's *desire* to support and engage in a particular solution. An argument can be made for creating awareness of the need for change even before a specific solution has been developed, especially when the need for change is external and observable.

Based on the research data, what would project teams do differently next time regarding communications with employees?

The following answer is an excerpt from Prosci's Best Practices in Change Management report.[2] When asked what they would do differently next time related to communications, participants in the study stated:

1. Communicate more frequently. Share messages more than you think you need to.

   "You can't over-communicate."

2. Find more effective ways to reach your audience.

   • Use multiple channels (meetings, one-on-one, newsletters, presentations, brainstorming workshops, lunch and learns, Intranet Q&A forums, CDs, screen-saver messages, etc.).

   "We actually did the communication part fairly well. Hardest thing was getting people to actually read it, so we constantly changed how and what we said."

- Develop two-way channels to improve feedback and involvement.

"Don't assume people understand."

- Increase one-on-one communication with those directly impacted by the change.

3. Design a formal communication plan tied to project deliverables. Determine what to share, when to share it, who the audience will be and how to deliver the message.

4. Involve the entire organization in the communication plan. Give careful consideration to the sender of the message. There are times when the CEO is the preferred sender (to create awareness of the need for change). Supervisors will be critical in sending messages to those most impacted. Project champions (avid supporters) can also be advocates to enlist support.

5. Prepare your management team to ensure a consistent message. Communication is not a one-time event, and individuals will need some time to accept and react to the changes as they are explained and implemented. Spend adequate time building awareness of the need for change, discussing the impact directly with individuals and highlighting the opportunities to come.

Summary

Awareness-building is a process that occurs over time. When multiple change management tactics are applied, a process results where:

- Key messages around awareness are brainstormed and discussed to create a common understanding among the project team and sponsor.

- Awareness messages are communicated to employees based on a well-developed communication strategy.

- The executive sponsor directly participates in the process of creating awareness of the need for change; a sponsorship coalition is created that reinforces this awareness message throughout the organization.

- Managers and supervisors at each level engage with their employees about the change and reinforce the messages from the executive sponsor.

- Employees have time to internalize the message and provide feedback.

- Managers and supervisors react to misinformation, discuss the change one-on-one with employees, and provide feedback to the change management team on gaps in the awareness-building process.

These steps form an iterative process that ultimately builds awareness of the need for change throughout an organization.

Chapter 9
Creating Desire

Ultimately *desire* is about personal choice. Even in circumstances of great pain or promising hope, the choices people make can appear to defy logic or be unpredictable. It is, perhaps, this uncertainty and lack of control over another person's desire to change that cause some leaders to disengage from this part of the change process.

Yet, the actions and words of managers and executive leaders have a tremendous influence on an employee's desire to support a business change. Even if managers and business leaders cannot dictate the decisions of their employees, they can greatly impact the process.

As a basic principle, managers must first view the task of creating *desire* as more than managing resistance. Adopting a "resistance management" focus can take a business leader down a trail of reactive management actions that often turn into firefighting and damage control. In other words, you should not introduce a change and then wait to identify those groups or individuals who are resistant to that change. Rather, you should adopt those strategies and tactics that have been used by effective leaders of change that are positive and proactive. Your goal is not to drag along the unwilling and uncaring, with all your attention focused on this minority. Your objective is to create energy and engagement around the change that produces momentum and support at all levels in the organization.

Recall the primary factors that influence desire as introduced in Chapter 3, including:

- The nature of the change

- The organizational context for the change

- An employee's personal situation

- What motivates them as an individual

This chapter examines the change management tactics that influence these factors for creating desire.

Tactic 1 –Effectively sponsor the change with employees

Tactic 2 –Equip managers to be change leaders

Tactic 3 –Assess risks and anticipate resistance

Tactic 4 –Engage employees in the change process

Tactic 5 –Align incentive programs

Tactic 1 – *Effectively sponsor the change with employees*

The top three roles and responsibilities of executive sponsors during change, as presented in Chapter 8, include:

- Participate actively and visibly throughout the project

- Build a coalition of sponsorship with peers and managers

- Communicate effectively with employees

These roles are not only needed to build awareness of the need for change, but are essential to create desire among employees to support and engage in the change.

Participate actively and visibly throughout the project

Too often executive sponsors engage early in projects and then move on to other business priorities. The role of sponsorship, however, is just as critical during implementation as it was during the launch of a project. Senior managers must be willing to interact on a personal level and be visible throughout the entire change process.

A senior manager for a government agency scheduled a face-to-face meeting with her managers and supervisors to review a new organization structure and strategy for the upcoming year. Some members of the leadership team were surprised that the supervisors and managers in attendance were criticizing the new direction. Despite complete and concise communications sent out months before the meeting, resistance to change was evident among many managers. When it became clear that forward progress was stalled, the senior executive changed the agenda. She requested that the group split up and document their specific objections in breakout sessions. Later she candidly addressed each objection, head-on and face-to-face. The discussions were not rushed nor were any questions out of bounds. She actively and visibly engaged in sponsoring the change. She was *present* to address the hard questions. The leadership team was surprised to find that by the end of the second day, much of the conversation had shifted from "This is why we should not do this change" to "What do I need to do to get my group on board?" In this example, the senior executive demonstrated active and visible sponsorship of the change.

If a sponsor, on the other hand, decides to disengage from a change or engages only at the beginning of the project, the momentum and support for the project will diminish over time. The consequences of this disengagement include greater resistance to the change from employees, slower adoption rates throughout the organization and in some cases failure of the project. These same effects can be seen when there is a change of leadership during the implementation of a major initiative.

Employees watch closely to see if the new leadership actively and visibly supports the change to determine if the change is still important.

Build a coalition of sponsorship with peers and managers

The second component of sponsorship that creates a *desire* to change among employees is the building of a sponsorship cascade or sponsorship coalition. A strong sponsor coalition creates engagement among senior and mid-level managers that generates a desire to change among supervisors and front-line employees. A weak sponsorship coalition allows resistance to grow in the organization without consequence or recourse.

An example of a weak sponsorship model was evident in a large manufacturing company that had multiple change initiatives occurring at the same time. They were encountering mixed acceptance of the changes between different divisions or departments. In some cases departments were on board and willing to engage. In other cases groups expressed extreme resistance. A sponsorship assessment was conducted by the project teams for each change. The term *sponsorship assessment* as used here represents an analysis of both the level of support and the sponsorship competency of all key business leaders involved in the change. For this particular assessment, the resulting diagrams appeared as organization charts shaded green, yellow and red.

Green represented managers who were supportive of the change and who were able to sponsor the change within their group. Yellow reflected all managers who were indifferent to the change or who did not possess the skills to sponsor the change. Red indicated managers who were opposed to the change and who were perceived as threats or barriers.

For many of the projects, red or yellow boxes occupied nearly 50% of the organization charts. The sponsorship coalitions were too weak to support the types of changes that were being deployed. This lack of sponsorship throughout the management ranks was visible in the lack of *desire* to change among employees. In other words, employees were following the lead of their direct management chain.

Persistent resistance to a change from one or two senior managers or from middle managers can undermine an otherwise strong sponsor coalition. In these cases, executive sponsors must manage this resistance proactively. Tolerating resistance from senior or mid-level managers creates a mindset that it is "OK" to opt out of the change or that there are no real consequences for resisting the change.

The term *sacrificial lamb* is often used when referring to the removal of a key manager who is demonstrating persistent and damaging resistance to a change. When resistance to change is persistent and the change is necessary for the success of the organization, definitive action is required. In many cases, managers who are demonstrating resistance over a long period of time are ready to move on anyway. What appears to be resistance to the change is often related to other personal and professional concerns.

Removing a resistant manager sends a powerful signal to the organization as a whole. The message is:

We are serious about this change.

Resistance will not be tolerated.

The consequences for not moving ahead are real and severe.

In most cases, the primary sponsor is in the best position to handle this type of situation with care and professionalism. Removal of a resistant manager is most effective when other employees and managers already see the damaging impacts or obstacles created by this individual's behavior. Taking action against a manager will set a precedent for the organization and should be used as a last resort for dealing with threatening resistance. Note that this action does not necessarily imply termination. In many cases managers can be moved to other jobs in the business. This provides them with a new start and removes the point of resistance for the change at the same time. Use this method with caution and with involvement of your Human Resource group and legal department.

Communicate effectively with employees and managers

Executive sponsors must communicate effectively with employees throughout the project. The sponsor plays a critical role in communicating those messages that employees want to hear from the person in charge:

- A vision of where the organization is going

- A roadmap that outlines how the vision will be achieved

- Clear alignment of the current change with this vision

- Specific goals or objectives that define success

- His or her personal commitment and passion for the change

Business leaders often underestimate their ability to create hope and to engage employees on an emotional level. They may underestimate the degree to which employees look to them for direction and leadership. In the book Primal Leadership: Learning to Lead with Emotional Intelligence, Daniel Goleman provides numerous examples of how leaders can effectively engage their employees at a level that captures their hearts and minds.[1] This leadership competency is a developed skill and is necessary for the process of creating hope within employees.

In addition to sharing their personal commitment to the change, executive sponsors should directly communicate the benefits of the change to employees. They should make clear connections between the objectives of the change and the overall direction of the business. Executive sponsors may want to share success stories or struggles from other departments or from early trials with the change. Employees want to hear about the challenges endured during the transition and how they were handled. They want to hear the good and the bad, the suffering and the rewards. They want to hear that success is possible and they want to learn from the mistakes of others. Most importantly, they want to hear the primary sponsor speak about the opportunities and benefits for the business as a whole.

Most common executive manager mistakes

The three roles described above for executive managers represent the type of sponsorship that creates desire among employees. However, business leaders do not always assume these roles. According to the 2005 Change Management study results,[2] the most common mistakes made by executive managers included:

Mistake #1 – Failed to engage personally as the sponsor for the change. Project teams reported that their sponsor:

- Abdicated sponsorship to lower-level managers, the project team or consultants

- Was absent or ignored the project; failed to stay involved and track progress; was not visible after the initial kick-off

- Failed to communicate the need for change and risk of not changing

- Failed to reinforce a consistent message; the sponsor was not visible and active throughout the entire project

Mistake #2 – Changed priorities mid-stream. Project teams reported that:

- Commitment wavered or support dwindled over time

- Other projects took priority

- The sponsor moved on to the next "flavor of the month"

Mistake #3 – Did not create a sponsorship coalition. Project teams stated that the sponsor:

- Assumed support from other business leaders would be there; moved too fast without ensuring that key managers were on board

- Underestimated resistance and the impact of the change on employees

- Assumed the message trickled down; assumed everyone understood the need for change

- Failed to set expectations of other business leaders

- Tolerated resistance from mid-level managers

These common mistakes by executive sponsors directly impact employees' desire to support and participate in a change. Executive managers who delegate the role of sponsorship or who are absent during the change process indirectly tell employees that this change is not very important. Executive managers who change priorities mid-stream send the message that "If you wait long enough, this too shall pass." Executive managers who fail to create a sponsor coalition will often see one or more managers not supporting the change. The employees who work under that chain of command will have less desire to support the change if their own manager is not on board.

Tactic 2 - *Equip managers and supervisors to be change leaders*

Employees ultimately turn to their immediate supervisor for direction. In order for supervisors to create desire within their employees, they need to:

- Conduct effective conversations about the change at a group and individual level

- Manage persistent resistance to the change

- Demonstrate commitment to the change through their behavior

A customer service manager was required to implement a process change in her call center to increase cross-selling of products. She met with each employee to discuss the change and provided general guidelines for how cross-selling would be initiated with customers. A training session was conducted that included role plays and scripts for the agents to use. Several weeks later the manager noticed that one agent in particular was not cross-selling to customers. The manager met face-to-face with the employee to talk about the issue. The conversation centered on the training scripts and methods for engaging customers. The manager left the meeting believing she really made an impact and did a good job training this employee. The performance data came out two weeks later. This agent was still not cross-selling. The manager decided that the employee did not have the ability to cross-sell products and decided to move this agent into a different role. When the agent found out that she was being moved out of her team, she immediately confronted her manager and asked for one more chance. The employee stated that she was unaware of the consequences associated with this change before now. The supervisor agreed and two more weeks passed. The manager was surprised to find out in the next reporting period that this agent had cross-sold more products than any other person on the team. Over time this agent repeatedly showed the best cross-selling performance of any team member.

In this case study, the supervisor erroneously started the conversation about change with her employees at the *knowledge* element of the ADKAR model (she began with training). She did not build awareness of why the change was needed nor did she assess the desire of this employee to support and participate in the change. When performance issues surfaced, she focused again on the *knowledge* for cross-selling. However, the agent that would not cross-sell lacked *desire*, not knowledge or ability. If the supervisor had taken the time to diagnose the barrier point to this change, she would have found out that this employee was uncomfortable pushing products onto customers. The agent was happy to take customer orders and hang up. It was not until the customer service agent faced the consequence of a reduced role, different from her colleagues, that she made a personal choice to support the change. The quality and content of the conversation with the employee had a direct impact on the success of the change.

Having the right conversations with employees

Conversation was deliberately chosen for naming this interaction between supervisors and their employees during change. Conversation in this context does not mean to debate, argue, present or persuade. It simply means to talk about the change.

A supervisor should be open to having conversations about all aspects of the change. Some employees may want to talk about past failed changes and why this change will be any different. Others may need to talk about their personal circumstances and how this change will affect them. Still others will want to debate the reasons a change is being made. All of these topics must be part of effective supervisors' conversations with employees. Supervisors should not assume that an employee will be resistant to the change. The purpose of the conversation is to allow the employee to sort out their questions and concerns over the change in a professional setting.

The process for enabling managers and supervisors to have effective conversations with their employees begins with managing the change with the supervisors first. When changes occur in an organization, a supervisor or manager is an employee first and manager second. In other words, they will have their own questions and potential issues with the change that must be resolved before they can effectively sponsor the change with employees. That means the project team and the executive sponsor must play an active role in managing change with supervisors and managers in the organization.

Managers and supervisors may also need training on change management. A common error is to assume that supervisors are by default effective coaches and change managers. The competency to manage change effectively with employees is a developed skill. The change management team in partnership with HR should ensure that training programs are in place to teach supervisors how to manage change, and when necessary, how to manage resistance.

Managing persistent resistance

Resistance to change from employees and managers is a common obstacle to successful change projects. The current state has a powerful hold on employees. In the parable told by Spencer Johnson in <u>Who Moved My Cheese?</u>, each character views the change in the cheese differently.[3] One character was so fearful of the unknown, that even in the face of starvation he resisted change.

In Prosci's 2005 Change Management report,[4] the top five reasons that employees resisted change as cited by study participants were:

1. Employees were not aware of the underlying business need for change.

2. Layoffs were announced or feared as part of the change.

3. Employees perceived the need for new skills that they currently lacked.

4. Individuals resisted the change in an attempt to maintain the personal rewards, sense of accomplishment and fulfillment provided by the current state.

5. Employees believed they were being required to do more with less, or more for the same pay.

The top five reasons that managers resisted change were:

1. Loss of power, responsibility or resources.

2. Overburdened with current responsibilities and workload.

3. Lacked awareness of the need for change.

4. Lacked the skills needed to manage the change – believed they were unprepared to manage the change with employees.

5. Felt fearful or uncertain about the changes being made.

Although this data provides a general understanding of the primary causes for resistance to a change, the data does not reveal why a particular individual may be resistant to a change. Therefore, several techniques can be used to identify and manage resistance from an employee.

Identify the barrier point to this change

To begin the process of managing resistance, a manager must first consider which elements or building blocks of the ADKAR model are currently strong or weak for an individual. In other words, what is the *barrier point* to change for this person? For example, you would not want to use resistance management steps that focus on *desire* if the barrier point for that employee was *knowledge* or *ability*. First assess where that person stands in terms of the ADKAR model. If *desire* is determined to be the barrier point to change, then the following techniques will be useful.

Listen and understand objections

A critical first step when creating desire to change is to stop talking and start listening. Supervisors and managers who are not skilled in managing resistance tend to begin with attempts at persuasion. If that does not work, they often resort to threats. Yet, in many cases employees simply want to be heard and to voice their objections. Understanding these objections can often provide a clear path toward resolution. It is useful to ask "What are your specific objections to this change?" or "What are your biggest concerns with this change?" and then to listen to the employee. Often the resistance is not about the change itself, but rather how the change will impact them personally.

Remove obstacles

Obstacles to change may relate to family, personal issues, physical limitations or money. Managers must fully understand the individual situation with this employee. What may appear to be resistance or objections to the change may be barriers that the employee cannot see past. Identify the obstacles clearly. Determine ways that the business may be able to address these personal barriers or assist the employee in thinking through solutions to these concerns.

A vice president for a public services company was resisting a change that involved moving to another role in the business. When the CEO asked point-blank what the barrier to change was, the VP responded that the work location for the new position would require an additional one-hour commute on top of his existing 45-minute drive. This would directly impact his ability to spend more time at his son's after-school activities, a recent commitment he had made to his family. The resistance to change in this example was not about the change, but the impact that change had on the employee's personal situation.

Too often managers do not solicit from employees their specific objections to the change in order to identify obstacles. Often these barriers can be removed without adversely impacting the change.

Make a personal appeal

Some managers can create a desire to change by making a personal appeal and leveraging their relationship with employees. A personal appeal works best with honest, open relationships where there is a high degree of trust and respect. A personal appeal from a supervisor may sound like:

I believe in this change.

It is important to me.

I would like your support.

You would be helping me by making this change work.

With this approach, the implied message is often that the supervisor will take care of or look out for the employee during the transition. Exercise caution when using this approach; make sure that you can follow through with this implied commitment.

Negotiate

In very special cases, such as acquisitions or mergers, resistance can be managed through a process of negotiation. In these circumstances the organization has decided that a particular person is essential for the transition and is willing to bargain with money or advancement to acquire his or her support. This could include increasing their compensation, offering a promotion to a position they desire or creating a bonus program so they are directly rewarded for the successful completion of the change. In some cases the person may be rewarded for staying with the company just through the transition, and then they receive a severance package that has been negotiated up front.

Provide simple, clear choices and consequences

Building desire is ultimately about choice. Managers can facilitate this process by being clear about the choices employees have during change. It is necessary to communicate in simple and clear terms what the choices and consequences are for each employee.

By providing simple and clear choices along with the consequences of those choices, managers can put the ownership and control back into the hands of employees. Desire to participate and support a change is an employee's decision that managers can enable by clearly stating the options.

Hold employees accountable

A business manager must be able to hold employees accountable for their performance as it relates to a change in the business – especially when resistance to a change is having a direct impact on the business and on other employees. Managers must be trained and empowered to use whatever means the organization has available to hold employees accountable for their actions and work performance in support of the change. Managers should understand the corrective action process and how they need to work with HR to resolve persistent performance issues.

Convert the strongest dissenters

Managers can also manage resistance on a group level by targeting a strong and vocal dissenter. A strong dissenter can become your strongest advocate. A strong dissenter can be as vocal in their support as they were in their resistance. For example, nearly 2000 years ago on the road to Damascus, Paul, one of the strongest persecutors of early Christians, became one of the most enduring and powerful evangelists for the early Christian church. You most likely know someone in your group or department who is the loudest complainer or the person who is always first to point out what is wrong. These individuals dominate the conversations at lunch or on breaks. When one-on-one time is invested with such individuals to address their resistance to change, these outspoken employees can become open advocates for the change, and their opinions can positively influence many other employees.

Managers and supervisors play a key role in building desire with employees. They are the center point for those critical conversations about a change. They remove barriers and manage resistance. Last, but certainly not least, managers and supervisors demonstrate commitment to the change through their own behavior. Their actions provide a visible model that can build strong support for the change.

Tactic 3 – *Assess risks and anticipate resistance*

A well-rounded change management approach includes a process for assessing risks and mitigating those risks to reduce resistance to the change. Most change management methods include readiness assessments to assist with this process. These assessment tools help identify potential problem areas before encountering resistance. By addressing these risks or gaps ahead of time, resistance in some cases can be avoided. This notion of proactively taking steps to prevent or lessen resistance to change is inherent in good change management approaches and directly impacts employees' desire to support a change. Two types of assessments are useful to determine risks and identify gaps:

- Change assessments

- Organizational readiness assessments

Change assessments evaluate the nature of the change from the perspective of the organization, and specifically from the perspective of different groups. Good change assessments evaluate the following elements:

- Scope of change (workgroup, department, division, enterprise)

- Number of impacted employees (identified for each impacted group)

- Variation in groups that are impacted (are all groups impacted the same or will groups experience the change differently?)

- Type of change (simple change, complex change)

- Degree of process, technology and job role change

- Degree of organization restructuring and changes to staffing levels

- Impact on employee compensation

- Time frame for the change (a few days, many years)

- Alignment of the change with the overall business vision and direction

The purpose of a change assessment is to develop an overall view of the size and scope of the change. This assessment evaluates the impact on different groups. By comparing the future state of the change with the current state, you can see the overall gap or transition that is required for different areas in the organization. When combined with an organizational readiness assessment, you can begin to identify potential areas of resistance and unique challenges for the organization.

Organizational readiness assessments are used to evaluate the overall readiness of the organization to change. Some organizations are change-resistant while others are change-ready. Good organizational assessments include:

- Impact of past changes (do employees perceive past changes as positive or negative?)

- Change capacity (are very few changes underway, or is everything changing?)

- Success of past changes (were past changes successful and well-managed, or did many projects fail and were changes poorly managed?)

- Shared vision and direction for the organization (is there a widely shared and unified vision, or are there many different directions and shifting priorities?)

- Resources and funding availability (are adequate resources and funds available, or are resources and funds limited?)

- Organization's culture and responsiveness to change (is the culture open and receptive to new ideas and change, or closed and resistant?)

- Organizational reinforcement (are employees rewarded for risk-taking and embracing change, or rewarded for consistency and stability?)

The combination of change assessments and readiness assessments allows you to evaluate the overall impact this change will have on the organization. This type of analysis can bring to the surface unique challenges for a specific group and will allow the project team to identify potential areas of resistance. For example, a change assessment may suggest a significant impact on the sales group, while the organizational readiness assessment indicates a culture and history in the sales division that is rigid and change-resistant. Special tactics will need to be developed to address the potential resistance in this area. In terms of creating *desire*, these change and organization assessments are proactive planning tools to identify and mitigate resistance early in the process.

Tactic 4 - *Engage employees in the change process*

The more you can engage employees in the change process, the greater their desire will be to support and participate in the change. For some types of changes, it is effective for managers to let go of the *how* and simply communicate *what* needs to change (focus on outcomes). It is not always necessary to tell employees exactly how to accomplish the change, but rather share the business objectives and let them determine how best to make that happen. This process transfers ownership of the solution to employees.

Employee involvement and ownership naturally build desire to support the change. Employees who are involved at the beginning are much more likely to be allies at the end. Participation creates passion and commitment to success.

As you consider the many different groups that will be impacted by the change, who are the movers and shakers in those groups? Who do people look to for the latest information? Who are the opinion leaders? Engaging these individuals will have a substantial impact on the overall success of the change.

There are several roles that employees can play in the change process. They may be invited to participate on the design team. In this capacity they are instrumental in developing the final solution. They may be invited to participate on the change management team. In this role they will serve as a spokesperson for their area and can help design change management strategies for their group. They may be part of trials or pilots of the new design, allowing the project team to solicit early feedback and input for improvement. Engaging employees in the change process is a very powerful way to build support.

Tactic 5 – *Align incentive programs*

If incentive programs are in place, they must be realigned to support the desired behavior. In the workplace, for example, salespeople may be compensated for meeting specific goals or objectives. If these goals or objectives are not aligned with the change, then the incentive to continue old behaviors remains in place. Recall that one of the factors influencing *desire* is "what's in it for me." If people determine that the change has a negative consequence for them because of the existing incentive programs, then their desire to change will be lower than if the old incentive programs were either removed completely or redesigned to support the change.

A change often requires updates to performance management systems as well. Even when financial compensation is not directly tied to the performance metrics, the behaviors of employees are strongly driven by how they are measured. If the measurement system is not aligned with the change, then employees may resist implementing changes that hinder their ability to meet their performance objectives.

Frequently asked questions related to desire

If employees support a change today, can you expect that they will always support the change?

Employees may respond positively to the general idea of change, especially if they see evidence that change is necessary in an organization. Later, they may resist that same change depending on how the change impacts them personally. Some employees may vacillate between support and opposition as they learn more about the nature of the change and "what's in it for me."

Is resistance to change normal and to be expected?

You may have heard the statement, "Resistance to change is normal." In general I believe this statement to be true. However, you have to be careful not to extend this statement to say, "People are resistant to change." As a collective group, we have shown ourselves to be quite adaptable over time. To understand why resistance from an individual reflects normal human behavior, you need to consider three different circumstances that a person may encounter. The first circumstance is one in which a person is comfortable with the current state. They have found success and happiness with the way things are today. They may have worked hard over a long period of time to create this circumstance. The second circumstance is one in which a person is opposed to the current state. They may be experiencing failure or oppression. They most likely see the current state as a contributor to their unhappiness and would be a strong proponent for change. The third circumstance is one of indifference or neutrality. A person in this circumstance may have little invested in the current state or may be new to a situation. In this case, this person is a bystander and observer of the events unfolding around them. If you find yourself in the first circumstance, then resistance to change would be expected and would be a natural reaction to change. However, if you are in the second circumstance, you may be the change advocate. How we react to change is largely rooted in our current circumstances.

Can incentives be used to create desire?

The answer depends on the individual. The notion that you can use a reward or penalty to influence desire is somewhat narrow in scope in that many factors influence a person's choices, not just the hope for gain or the fear of loss. Not all individuals can be motivated by financial incentives. For example, in situations where a person perceives a conflict between their values and the values of the organization, they typically would not respond to financial incentives. It is more effective to understand what is important to that individual through effective coaching, and then to build desire around those things that are meaningful to that person.

Who is the best person to manage resistance from a mid-level manager?

Resistance from mid-level managers is cited as the most common area for resistance to change. Often mid-level managers have the most to lose, as they see their power or control erode in many types of change. Consider their position for a moment. They do not make strategic decisions nor do they perform the direct, day-to-day operational tasks. They typically manage people and budgets. Their span of control is directly tied to those they manage and the associated finances to run those operations. When changes are introduced that shift people or money, then some mid-level managers will gain control while others will lose. Some may see change as a reflection on their success, while others perceive change as a statement of failure. Many of these changes will impact careers. As a result, resistance from some mid-level managers is very common. Given the political nature of this level of management, only their direct supervisor or a senior manager in the chain of command can manage their resistance to change. In some cases, the primary sponsor may be in the role to assist with this process.

How do you teach change management to managers who are resistant to the change itself?

Some project teams that are implementing change find it difficult to train managers and supervisors in change management when they are in the middle of a major change initiative. This quandary is understandable. Why would a manager who is resistant to a change want to learn how to manage that change effectively with their employees? The solution to this problem is to separate the task into two parts. First, manage the change with the managers and supervisors. They must have awareness of the need for change and a desire to participate in the change. Second, teach them how to manage change with their employees. Anytime you put training or *knowledge* ahead of *awareness* and *desire* you will be disappointed with the results; conversely, whenever *awareness* and *desire* are present, an individual naturally seeks the *knowledge* of how to succeed.

Summary

Multiple tactics can be used to create *desire* to support and participate in a change. Sponsorship by executive leaders is instrumental in this process. Executive sponsors influence desire by:

- Participating actively and visibly through the entire change process

- Building coalitions of sponsorship with key business managers

- Communicating directly to employees and by creating energy and hope around the future state

Managers and supervisors influence desire by helping employees make sense of the change. They are instrumental in communicating "what's in it for me" and talking through the change with each employee. They are the translators. They help employees understand the change as it relates to their personal situation and what is important to them as individuals. Managers and supervisors are the front line when it comes to managing persistent and threatening resistance. They must have the tools to act appropriately with employees who refuse to support the change.

Readiness assessments help the change management team identify potential problem areas and devise special tactics that will proactively avoid resistance before problems arise. This process also helps change management teams understand the political climate and magnitude of the task at hand.

Employee engagement in the change process allows employees to participate in the design, development, testing and implementation of the final solution. Nothing builds desire faster than direct participation and ownership for the change.

Incentive programs and performance management systems must be aligned with and supportive of the change. Behavior is strongly influenced by how people are measured and rewarded.

The most successful change initiatives focus their efforts on the proactive steps that sponsors and managers can take to create energy and engagement around the change. Resistance is managed not as the primary activity, but as one component in a larger strategy to create desire.

Chapter 10

Developing Knowledge

Developing *knowledge* is a primary activity for most project teams. They view training to be instrumental in the success of new processes, systems and job roles. In fact, some project team leaders would jump right to this topic with little consideration for the prior elements of the ADKAR model. Unfortunately, skipping right to *knowledge* has many implications for a project's success.

This potential pitfall is best illustrated with a case study. A customer service call center received millions of service calls each year from customers. During a major redesign of the call center's processes and systems, two initiatives emerged that would dramatically reduce the overall cost of operations.

The first initiative was a move toward customer self-service using automated telephone systems to answer frequently asked questions and to allow customers to check the status of their service orders without talking to agents. The more calls that could be handled by the automated system, the less time agents would have to spend handling these requests.

The second initiative was to introduce a knowledge-base system for all call center employees. This system would enable employees to handle a wide range of customer problems and to solve more complex issues. The knowledge-base system would provide search capability, easy access to trouble-shooting data and would allow the agents to contribute new information to the system each day. The result was a system that would become "smarter" and more valuable the more it was used.

A different team was assigned to each initiative. For the customer self-service initiative, this team began thinking through their strategy for implementation by evaluating the customer base and considering which customers would use the automated system and which would not. They also considered the fact that customers' use of the system would probably start out low and then would increase as time went by. They understood that not all customers would feel comfortable with a menu-driven phone system. As they developed the business case for the new system, assumptions were made regarding total use of the system in the first year, the second year and so on through a five-year deployment. These assumptions helped them develop a realistic financial projection of the total savings over time.

When the customer self-service team began implementation of the system, their starting point was building awareness with customers. Communications focused on creating awareness that a new application was available. Over time, brochures, billing information and recorded messages began to focus on the benefits to the customers of choosing self-service. The team began their deployment with a focus on the first two elements of the ADKAR model, *awareness* and *desire*. They understood that the customer was ultimately in control. It was the customer's choice to use the system or to opt out and speak to an agent. As the new system was deployed, their projections and assumptions about customer usage were surprisingly accurate. Over time the business realized substantial cost savings from this initiative.

The knowledge-base team began their strategy for implementation with a carefully crafted training program for employees. They viewed *knowledge* of the new system as the success factor for their initiative and wanted to be sure that employees were adequately prepared for the cutover of the new knowledge-base tool. As they prepared their business case, the primary focus was on the cost savings per call that would be realized once the tool was in place. They assumed all employees would use the new application.

After the new system was fully deployed, the team was surprised to find out that some call center agents were not using the new tool and that other agents used the tool infrequently.

What happened? The knowledge-base team focused on very different elements of the ADKAR model. They began with *knowledge* and *ability*. They assumed that all employees would fully utilize the new tool once it was deployed. The knowledge-base team assumed that "if you build it, they will use it." The unspoken assumption this team also made is that employees do not have a choice.

The customer self-service team, on the other hand, started with *awareness* and *desire*. They made the assumption that the customer had a choice and that the level of use would vary over time. They assumed that they needed to build awareness and desire with the customer so that they would choose to use the new self-service tool.

Each team made very different assumptions about the acceptance of the change by their respective audiences. The key lesson from this case study is that *knowledge* is not the starting point for managing change. Training by itself is not the answer. Attempts to build knowledge are effective only when the "students of change" want to engage in the change process and are seeking knowledge to help them be successful. Awareness and desire cannot be taken for granted, even in cases where the change impacts a captive audience, namely, employees that work for a company.

Creating knowledge with employees during change has other challenges for project teams. Adult learning is a complex area and is an essential foundation for developing knowledge in the workplace. Adults want to know why the topics being taught are important and relevant to them. If they cannot connect the knowledge offered during the training to an immediate problem, then both attention to the subject and retention of knowledge can decline.[1] Moreover, if employees are not yet ready to learn and are attending the training because their supervisor required attendance, then not only do they not connect the learning to a business problem, they may not want to be in the class at all.

Adults also remember only a fraction of the training, depending on how the knowledge transfer process is conducted. Research indicates that adults retain only a small fraction of what they read, slightly more of what they hear, and about one-half of what they observe in demonstrations. The highest retention modes result from the hands-on application of the learning to an immediate problem.[2]

Most change leaders or project team members are not skilled in adult learning processes and are not professional trainers or educators. Yet, project teams must provide knowledge on the required skills and behaviors in order for the change to be successful. In many cases the project team will benefit by using professional training developers and instructors to support these programs.

The following section outlines some of the most commonly used tactics for developing knowledge.

Tactic 1 – Effective training and education programs

Tactic 2 – Job aides

Tactic 3 – One-on-one coaching

Tactic 4 – User groups and forums

Tactic 1 – *Effective training and education programs*

Training programs are a primary channel for creating *knowledge,* but must be properly designed and delivered. In a business setting, training programs should include hands-on activities and demonstrations with less focus on lecture time and reading. Audio programs, web-based seminars and other multi-media programs should all be considered as viable ways to develop knowledge, but be aware of the limitations of these types of programs compared to hands-on activities. Concepts can be conveyed with multimedia channels, but retention around tools and processes will be highest when these tools are discussed and applied during the learning program.

When designing training programs, an assessment of the knowledge gaps that exist between the current state and the future state will need to be completed. This gap analysis illustrates what is missing between what people do today and what they will have to do tomorrow. This is a normal part of the training development process. However, understanding the knowledge required for making the transition is equally important and often overlooked. Rarely do changes simply happen as an event. During the transition, many old processes and systems will need to be used concurrently with the new processes and systems. Problems will likely arise that do not match what employees learned in training. Training requirements and the resulting training programs should address how to operate in the future state and how to transition to a new way of doing work.

A useful technique for assessing gaps between the current state and future state is to write new job descriptions for employees. The new job descriptions should detail the knowledge and skills needed to perform that role both during and after the transition. With the direct involvement of supervisors, these job descriptions can be used as a tool to determine the knowledge and skill gaps between the current state and the future state. HR can play a vital role in this process.

Finally, time the training to be as near to implementation as possible. Remember that retention will drop off sharply as more time passes between learning new skills and applying those skills in a real situation.

Tactic 2 – *Job aides*

Many types of knowledge content go beyond what people can easily remember. Job aides such as checklists and templates enable employees to follow more complex procedures. For system implementations, online help files and scripts serve this same role. These job aides could be in the form of paper documentation or quick-reference cards. When integrated into system software, job aides can be made context-sensitive, similar to how some popular software companies use their animated assistants to provide tips and help. Knowledge-base systems or trouble-shooting systems that offer online help tools are also useful ways to provide job aides to employees.

Tactic 3 – *One-on-one coaching*

Even with the most effective training programs, most employees need one-on-one coaching. Because individuals learn in different ways and at different paces, one-on-one coaching allows a trainer to provide customized education based on the unique obstacles faced by that individual. In some cases, the barrier to learning may not be related to the content, but to other issues. When formal training is over, this "trainer" is often the employee's direct supervisor.

For example, when a marketing company deployed new desktop software, the learning curve for some senior editors appeared to be very long. After sitting down with one of these editors, the supervisor noticed that this person typed with only two fingers and rarely used the mouse. Since the new application required advanced PC skills, including keyboarding and mouse aptitude, this editor was having difficulty learning the new software because of their low proficiency in typing and using the mouse. The barrier to developing knowledge was not related to the subject content of the new system at all, but rather a unique personal obstacle for this individual.

For one-on-one coaching to be a success, supervisors or designated mentors need to be equipped to serve in this capacity. In-depth training or previous experience with the change is needed. You want to ensure that the knowledge transferred by the coaches is correct and complete. If this is not possible with your current managers, then one-on-one coaching can be accomplished by providing access to experts on the change. These experts could be from the training group or they could be from outside the organization. They also could be expert users from another part of the organization.

A franchise submarine sandwich restaurant provided an excellent example of the use of experienced employees to coach new hires. I personally experienced a new employee who was interrupted by a fellow employee when my sandwich was being made incorrectly. Instead of reprimanding the new employee, a co-worker stopped what he was doing, demonstrated the technique to the new employee and then explained why it was done that way. As a customer I certainly did not mind the additional 30 seconds the process took, and appreciated having my sandwich made correctly. Moreover, I was pleased to hear additional questions from the new employee that were answered patiently and in such a way that I thought it was just part of the normal process of doing business.

One-on-one coaching will be critical to your training program. In many cases, employees are taking the training course weeks or months before they will personally implement the change. Knowledge can be forgotten over time. Knowles found that there is a time perspective as people mature in terms of retention of knowledge. In other words, the older we get, the greater the need for immediacy of implementation after training.[1] Because not all training classes can be provided in a "just-in-time" mode, one-on-one coaching provides immediate transfer of knowledge at the time of implementation.

Tactic 4 – User groups and forums

Learning from peers can be very powerful. Employees identify with and can relate to the experiences of their fellow workers.

User groups and forums are a channel for employees to teach one another. System implementations often use the concept of "super-users" to designate a collection of employees who have mastered the implementation of the tools and can teach others. These super-users typically have their own forum for sharing, and organize forums for other employees that are new to the implementation.

For example, call centers often use agent forums to share knowledge about new systems, processes or tools. Within these forums, call center agents share their experiences, how they handled different situations and how the tools assisted them. One vendor was surprised to learn that the agent forum actually identified more shortcuts for moving from one screen to another than the vendor knew existed. The agent forum provided a robust and ongoing education process that augmented what they had learned in training.

User groups and forums capitalize on experiential learning of employees. Experiential learning is much more effective to adult learners. Merriam and Caffarella[3] note that adults accumulate a growing reservoir of experience that is a rich resource of learning. User groups and forums can tap into this resource and empower employees to be part of the learning process.

Developing a solid knowledge foundation for your change will require a combination of traditional training, job aides, one-on-one coaching and effective peer mentoring. When used together, these techniques allow employees to develop knowledge and apply that knowledge in a just-in-time mode to support the change.

Frequently asked questions regarding knowledge

Is the term knowledge in the ADKAR model the same as training?

Knowledge as used in the ADKAR model refers only to the information and understanding on how to change. Training programs, on the other hand, commonly include hands-on applications and simulations that facilitate ability. In other words, well-designed training includes knowledge transfer and the practice needed to apply this new knowledge to real situations.

Can the development of knowledge cause someone to lose desire to support the change?

Newly acquired knowledge about the skills and behaviors needed to support a change could negatively influence an employee's desire to engage in that change, but this is more likely to occur when the employees were not well-informed about the nature of the change and "what's in it for me" in the first place. In other words, the coaching process failed to build awareness. If employees learn for the first time how the change will impact them in a training class, then they may change their mind about supporting the change. Training should not be used as a substitute for good coaching from their direct supervisor.

What is the difference between knowledge and ability?

Knowledge represents the cognitive understanding of specific information about the change, as well as an understanding, at an intellectual level, about how to change. *Ability* is the demonstrated capability to implement the change. For example, I may know how the game of tennis is played after watching a tennis video or by taking a class taught by a tennis professional, but that does not mean I will be a good tennis player. Teenagers may understand the fundamentals of driving a car based on a "safe-driving" program, but that does not make them good drivers. *Ability* is the transformation of knowledge into action to achieve the desired performance within the organization.

Summary

Developing knowledge requires a broad spectrum of activities that enable each person to learn in a way that is most effective for them. These activities should include:

- Formal training and education programs

- Job aides that are available in real time once employees are back on the job

- One-on-one coaching from supervisors or subject matter experts

- User groups and forums (peer groups to share lessons learned)

Chapter 11
Fostering Ability

Developing abilities related to new processes, tools and job roles will vary from employee to employee. Some will fall naturally into the new way of work, while others may struggle.

Managers who use training programs as their primary change management tool might assume that *knowledge* automatically leads to *ability*. There are two common pitfalls that can occur with managers who believe that implementing change is equivalent to conducting training. First, training can be ineffective if the trainees were not *aware* that a change was needed or have no *desire* to support the change. Second, training employees does not always lead to the *ability* to act in a new way or to use new processes or tools. Knowing how to do something and being able to do something are not necessarily the same thing. Recall the potential barriers for ability covered in Chapter 5, including psychological barriers, physical limitations, intellectual capability, availability of resources and time.

Several tactics can be used to develop the abilities of employees in a changing environment.

Tactic 1 – Day-to-day involvement of supervisors

Tactic 2 – Access to subject matter experts

Tactic 3 – Performance monitoring

Tactic 4 – Hands-on exercises during training

Tactic 1 – *Day-to-day involvement of supervisors*

Supervisors play an important coaching role with their employees at this phase of change. By coaching employees one-on-one, a supervisor can readily identify the gaps in ability of their associates. Many employees need hands-on demonstrations or need someone to role model the change. Employees also need to know that if they attempt to work in new ways and fail, there will not be adverse consequences for them. This is where the supervisor has a tremendous impact with employees in terms of setting the stage for change. Developing ability takes time and practice. There must be a safe environment to practice new skills and job roles, and someone to provide correction, coaching and support.

This process begins with supervisors making their employees aware that implementing change takes time and practice, and that mistakes or missteps are part of the learning process. Supervisors must then encourage employees to implement the new changes, even if the process does not work perfectly the first time. Supervisors must establish a safe way for employees to seek help and to provide feedback when the change is not happening as expected. By keeping these channels open, managers can determine quickly when the breakdowns are related to ability of the employee or related to something else about the change. For example, a new system may have software problems or a new process may not account for special circumstances that the employee encounters. If the feedback channel is not open, then the employee will appear to be failing when the system is actually at fault.

Supervisors may not understand the level or depth of their role in managing change. Training for supervisors is critical if you expect them to take on this coaching role. As it relates to ability, you must prepare them for the following activities:

- How to provide one-on-one coaching of employees who are implementing new processes, tools and job roles;

supervisors should be able to provide demonstrations and to role model the desired ability

- How to create a safe environment that allows employees to practice and to make mistakes without retribution

- How to create feedback channels to the change management team to identify gaps in processes or tools

Tactic 2 – *Access to subject matter experts*

Subject matter experts are also useful at this stage of change. Beyond providing knowledge about the change, subject-matter experts or employees experienced with the change can provide direct assistance to other employees. The key to making this work is letting employees know whom to go to for help. Some companies set up a help desk where employees can call with questions. Others provide the names and contact information for mentors or subject matter experts.

What is difficult to ascertain during this phase of the change process is whether the barrier to change is ability or incomplete knowledge about the change. Many employees do not learn until the task is immediately in front of them. The access to experts, mentors and their own supervisor may be filling a knowledge gap more than developing ability. Since each person has to develop the ability on their own, these resources are simply there to assist in that process. For example, if you watch a person learn how to type (develop keyboarding skills), then you can appreciate that you can only do so much to help them. Eventually people just need time to practice, make mistakes and find out what works for them.

Tactic 3 – *Performance monitoring*

Measurement and performance assessments also play a key role in developing ability. The organization needs to know if the change is being implemented as designed, and employees need feedback on what they are doing well and what areas need improvement. In the absence of measurement and performance assessment, you may never know if employees are developing the right abilities or if the change is taking hold correctly. Many changes stall when problems occur that do not fit the training provided to employees. In these cases, employees either make up new procedures or revert to what they did before. Measurement and performance assessments help supervisors and project team members understand where the change is succeeding and under what circumstances the change is failing.

Tactic 4 – *Hands-on exercises during training*

In addition to providing knowledge to employees, effectively designed training programs should include hands-on activities that allow employees to test their new-found knowledge in different work scenarios. Role plays, simulations and actual hands-on work with new tools and processes allow employees to develop abilities in a controlled environment. Take the example of someone learning how to golf by watching an instructional video compared to playing golf side-by-side with the local golf pro. Actually applying knowledge to different situations that reflect the real work environment can accelerate the process of developing abilities.

Frequently asked questions about ability

Is it possible that poor performance (low ability) is actually disguised resistance to the change?

Work slowdowns and poor work performance could be disguised forms of resistance to the change. Care should be taken to evaluate the situation with each employee on a one-on-one basis. When trained in change management, supervisors will be able to distinguish one from another and implement corrective action.

What do you do with employees who cannot perform in the new environment?

Recall the example provided about the call center agent who was a poor performer in terms of cross-selling product. In this case, the supervisor made a mistake by assuming that *knowledge* or *ability* was the problem. In fact, it turned out that *desire* was the barrier point. When employees are not performing in the new environment, the first step is to validate where they are in the ADKAR model and address the first weak area (identified as the barrier point). If that area is *ability*, then consider how much time has been allowed for the employee to develop new skills. What additional support could be provided to help them make the transition? Remember that change is a process. Some employees will need more time than others. If your corrective action process is not successful over time, then this employee may need to move to another position or seek other opportunities outside of the organization.

Summary

Ability is the demonstrated capability to implement the change at the desired performance level. Ability is not equivalent to knowledge and is not an automatic outcome of training programs. Project teams should implement several channels to assist employees in the process of developing abilities, including:

- Day-to-day involvement of supervisors (so that a coaching relationship is established that creates a safe environment to learn new skills and behaviors)

- Access to subject matter experts (to close knowledge gaps and to have one-on-one demonstrations)

- Performance monitoring (so that demonstrated progress is measured against the desired outcomes for the change)

- Hands-on exercises during training (to provide practice before trying new processes or tools on the job)

Chapter 12
Reinforcing Change

Reinforcement is the final element of the ADKAR model and is achieved when the necessary mechanisms are in place to sustain the change.

With effective reinforcement, you avoid losing momentum from the initial deployment of the change and you can prevent employees from reverting to old ways of doing work. By building reinforcement mechanisms, the probability that project objectives are met increases dramatically.

An example of a failed change that resulted from a lack of reinforcement occurred with a bank that was attempting to deploy quality-improvement tools and processes throughout their entire organization. The project was started by the information systems vice president. He formed a cross-functional team from departments throughout the business. After an extensive selection process, his team chose a methodology and tool set. The team carefully crafted a project plan and followed that plan to the letter. Executive business leaders were engaged to sponsor the change. The training department created a training curriculum with the help of an outside vendor. The IT group put tools and resources online. The IT vice-president effectively communicated the need for quality tools to employees and other senior business leaders.

When the training program was initially deployed, the implementation team provided direct oversight for the program. They managed the communications and orchestrated each training event. They worked actively to "sell" the need for quality tools and processes across the organization. The implementation was going well. Classes were full. The program was working.

Then a critical error was made. Early in the implementation, the project team disbanded. The program was transferred to an existing staff group responsible for quality in manufacturing. The training group added this quality improvement program to their standard courses and treated it like business as usual. The course became part of an open enrollment program. Within one year of disbanding the team, six courses had been cancelled. Interest in the program had evaporated and, for all practical purposes, the program was dead.

What happened in this case study can happen to any change that lacks reinforcement. The first mistake the implementation team made was to assume that managing change is essentially completing activities in a project plan. They completed the plan and disbanded without ensuring that the change had taken hold and that reinforcement mechanisms were in place. They failed to assess the progress of the change and to take the pulse of the organization after deployment was underway. They did not create processes for ongoing accountability. Measurement systems were not in place to evaluate success. Corrective action was not implemented to address problems that surfaced. Sponsorship that was strong at the onset faded in the time of greatest need. Recognition and reward programs were absent. The change was not cemented into the organization's culture or value system. This was a prescription for failure.

Several tactics for building *reinforcement* are described below. These are certainly not the only tactics for sustaining change, and your team should consider which methods would have the best result for your situation. They include:

Tactic 1 – Celebrations and recognition

Tactic 2 – Rewards

Tactic 3 – Feedback from employees

Tactic 4 – Audits and performance measurement systems

Tactic 5 – Accountability systems

Tactic 1 – *Celebrations and recognition*

Managers and supervisors play a key role in recognizing employees and celebrating successes. Employees view their direct supervisor as a preferred sender in the change process, and these managers are in the best position to recognize employees in a meaningful way. Supervisors have a variety of tools at their disposal to accomplish this task. The biggest mistake most supervisors make is that they simply forget this step or become busy with other tasks.

The first and easiest way for supervisors to recognize employees is by one-on-one conversations that are informal and private. This is also one of the most effective methods. The supervisor should acknowledge the change that was made, the effort it took to make the change and what results they are seeing. They should directly thank the employee for their support and hard work throughout the change process. The goal of this recognition is to make the employee feel genuinely appreciated for their contribution to the change.

The second method is public recognition. This approach is useful to acknowledge outstanding performance and for creating a role model for the change. Care must be taken if selecting only a few individuals for recognition. The risk is that a supervisor may alienate other employees who believe they have done as much as, or more than, the person being recognized.

The third method is through group celebrations. A supervisor should seek out activities or events that are fun for the group and that serve as a celebration for key milestones associated with the change. Examples include small events such as a pizza lunch to large events such as a group outing to a sporting activity.

The primary sponsor also plays a key role in the reinforcement process for successful change. This is not a responsibility that can or should be delegated. The primary sponsor of change must publicly recognize the achievement of key phases of the change with as much vigor as when he or she initiated the change. Employees look to the person in charge to share the ultimate outcomes of the change and to celebrate that achievement. Employees view the lead executive as a preferred sender and the best person to convey the nature of the change for the business. Employees also want to hear from this leader when success has been achieved. Celebrations are counter-culture for some organizations. The primary sponsor must find ways to publicly celebrate the change in a way that is meaningful to employees.

The primary sponsor should also be looking for short-term successes – those quick wins that occur early in the change process. If these early successes are celebrated and recognized, then the momentum for change builds. If they are ignored, then energy around the change can fade. In some ways the celebration of these early successes must be exaggerated to demonstrate recognition of the desired behavior and to create role models for the change.

Tactic 2 – *Rewards*

Rewards can be used to reinforce change under certain circumstances. In many cases you can identify performance objectives that, if met, would result in rewards for employees. In the case study with the customer service call center agent who was having trouble cross-selling products, the incentive was monetary. They were offered 15% of the incremental revenue for every product cross-sold to customers. This served as a reinforcing mechanism that directly rewarded the agent's ability to sell more products.

If monetary bonuses or incentives were offered early in the process as a resistance management tool or to build motivation for the change, then it is critical that managers follow through with these commitments. The process of awarding these incentives should be similar to non-monetary recognition. The manager should acknowledge the effort of the employee and the hard work associated with the transition. They should thank the employee for their contribution to the change and to the organization's success.

Some people ask if incentives are a *reinforcement* device or a method for building *desire*. The answer to this question depends on when the incentive is offered. If the incentive was offered as a method to solicit support and engagement, then the purpose of the incentive was to create desire. If the incentive is offered as a result of employees successfully implementing the change, then the focus is on reinforcement. Typically, incentives that focus on reinforcement are better termed "rewards" since their purpose is to affirm and reward something that has already been accomplished.

Tactic 3 – *Feedback from employees*

Part of reinforcing change is to understand how employees are reacting to the change. You would probably be surprised how often project teams never ask employees how they are doing with the change after initial implementation. Project teams commonly fail to gather data from employees. This process of gathering feedback through interviews, focus groups or surveys can help the project team understand where the change is taking hold and where the change is struggling.

Tactic 4 - *Audits and performance measurement systems*

Compliance audits and performance measurement systems are essential tools to determine the adoption rate of the change.

These tools could be based on system usage data, process check-lists or other measurement systems related to outputs from the changed process or system. Compliance audits should not be viewed as a negative activity on the part of the project team. You should be proactive in understanding how many employees are using the new processes or systems. What is their level of proficiency with these new processes or tools? What fraction of employees are not engaging in the change at all? How many employees are struggling with the change? What is the root cause for low adoption rates or non-compliance?

Only by completing formal assessments and reviewing performance data will you know if the change is taking hold. Armed with this data, the project team can determine the root cause of failure and implement corrective action.

Tactic 5 – *Accountability systems*

Effective changes include building accountability into normal business operations. If a change is implemented and no associated changes are made to performance evaluation programs or compensation systems, then the change lacks accountability. If a change has objectives to improve performance, these must be integrated into the quarterly or annual objectives of managers. Failure to build accountability into the system removes the ongoing element of reinforcement.

Building accountability into the system essentially means that leaders and managers in the business have assumed responsibility for the change and that they are held directly accountable for its success. This transfers accountability from the project team back to the business. If a change is to be sustained and fully realized, accountability must reside with day-to-day business operations and the associated managers in that business.

Frequently asked questions about reinforcement

What reinforcement techniques are the most effective?

The most effective reinforcement technique is dependent on the person and the situation. What is most important is that the reinforcement and recognition process is meaningful to the individual. Prosci's research indicates that in many cases the most effective reinforcement technique is the personal expression of appreciation by an employee's direct supervisor. In other cases, active and visible reinforcement by the executive sponsor is necessary.

Can some types of reinforcement backfire?

Some actions you could take to reinforce the change can have no effect or the opposite effect. For example, providing irrelevant rewards, like a DVD player to someone who does not watch TV, may not be seen as reinforcing to that employee. Recognizing one individual when an entire team contributed to the success may also have a negative effect on those not recognized for their contribution. The best reinforcements are those actions, words or rewards that are meaningful and equitable to that person or group.

What about customers? Does this process apply to them as well?

Although customers have not been explicitly named in every chapter as an audience for change, the building blocks for change as described by the ADKAR model apply equally to customers and suppliers. For changes in the government sector, the public is also an audience for change. For changes in our school system, teachers, parents and students are all impacted and will need to achieve each element of the ADKAR model if these changes are to be successful.

Summary

Reinforcing change is just as critical as that first communication to build awareness of the need for change. Reinforcement is that process of "pushing down the home stretch" and finishing the change. In short, reinforcing change can be any event that strengthens and sustains the change, including:

- Celebrations and recognition (even recognition of small successes)

- Rewards (that are relevant and meaningful)

- Feedback from employees

- Audits and performance measurement

- Accountability systems (to sustain the change over a long period of time)

Chapter 13

ADKAR
Enabling Elements Summary

The previous five chapters presented methods or tactics that can be used to achieve each element of the ADKAR model. A summary of these tactics is provided below. This summary is not intended to prescribe a process or set of steps for managing change. The methods presented in this book for achieving elements of the ADKAR model are not meant to be an exhaustive or complete list. The goal of these chapters was to demonstrate the alignment of commonly used change management activities like communications, coaching, training, sponsorship and resistance management with the respective goal or objective that should result from these activities. The ADKAR model provides a goal-oriented framework for these change management activities.

Building Awareness

1. Develop effective and targeted *communications* to share the business reasons for the change and the risk of not changing.

2. *Sponsor (lead)* the change effectively at the right level in the organization; share why the change is needed and how the change aligns with the overall business direction and vision.

3. Enable managers and supervisors to be effective *coaches* during the change process; prepare them to manage change and help them to reinforce awareness messages with their employees.

4. Provide employees with *ready access* to business information.

Creating Desire

1. Enable business leaders to effectively *sponsor* the change; create a *coalition of sponsorship* at key levels in the organization.

2. Equip *managers* and *supervisors* to be effective change leaders; enable them to manage resistance.

3. Assess the *risks* associated with the change and design special tactics to address those risks.

4. *Engage employees* in the change process at the earliest possible stages of the change.

5. *Align incentive and performance management systems* to support the change.

Developing Knowledge

1. Implement effective *training* and education programs.

2. Use *job aides* that assist employees in the learning process.

3. Provide one-on-one *coaching*.

4. Create *user groups* and forums to share problems and lessons learned between peer groups.

Fostering Ability

1. Foster the day-to-day involvement of *supervisors.*

2. Provide access to *subject-matter experts.*

3. Implement programs for *performance monitoring.*

4. Provide *hands-on exercises* during training that allow employees to practice what they have learned.

Reinforcing Change

1. *Celebrate* successes and implement recognition programs.

2. Give *rewards* for the successful implementation of the change.

3. Gather *feedback* from employees.

4. Conduct *audits* and develop *performance measurement systems*; identify root causes for low adoption and implement corrective action.

5. Build *accountability* mechanisms into the normal day-to-day business operations.

Figure 13-1 highlights the primary players and activities that contribute to each element of the ADKAR model.

ADKAR Elements	Who? The most influential players	How? The most influential activities
Awareness of the need for change	Primary sponsors (business leaders), Direct supervisors	Sponsorship (leadership), Communications, Coaching
Desire to support and participate in the change	Primary sponsors, Sponsor coalition, Direct supervisors	Sponsorship, Coaching, Resistance management
Knowledge of how to change	Project team, Training team, HR	Training, Coaching
Ability to implement required skills and behaviors	Direct supervisors, Project team, HR, Training team	Coaching, Training
Reinforcement to sustain the change	Primary sponsors, Direct supervisors	Sponsorship, Coaching

Figure 13-1 Relationship of change management activities to ADKAR

Chapter 14

ADKAR Applications

A DKAR is a model for enabling change. ADKAR provides a goal-oriented framework that helps change leaders realize their objectives more quickly and completely. Applications for the model include:

- A learning tool for teaching change management, especially when analyzing case studies of successful and failed changes

- A tool for change management teams to assess the readiness of their change management plans and guide their activities

- A coaching tool for managers and supervisors during change

- An assessment tool for diagnosing changes underway and identifying potential barrier points to change

- A planning tool for change

AKDAR as a device for teaching change management

ADKAR can be used as a helpful teaching tool for change management. The following case study illustrates how classroom discussions can be guided by the ADKAR model.

When national health care reform for the US was attempted in the 1990s under the Clinton administration, tremendous energy was focused on developing the "right" health care program. "Casts of hundreds" provided input and guidance into writing the final proposal. Despite the energy and time invested by the policy reform team to prepare the best reform plan, the change failed. In his article *What Happened to Health Care Reform?*, Paul Starr states:

> *... not just the Clinton plan was defeated. Every other proposal--the Cooper, Chafee, Moynihan, Mitchell, Cooper and Grandy, and mainstream group plans, to mention only the most prominent, consensus-building efforts--died in Congress.*[1]

As a member of the health policy team, Starr was at the epicenter of this story. He tells of political maneuvering and strategies by both Democrats and Republicans that moved health care reform initially forward and then irreversibly backward toward the ultimate demise of health care reform under the Clinton administration.

What is of interest in this case study is that failure came from an erosion of support, not a lack of knowledge. In the end, every proposal failed, even those from both sides of the aisle in Congress. The focus was on creating the "right" reform plan. The cause of failure, however, was rooted in lack of desire, not a lack of knowledge around the reform effort.

Starr writes that two particular factors may have influenced the overall perception and mood toward health care reform. First, health care was overshadowed by other priorities for the Clinton administration, including the economy and winning approval for his budget during the early part of his term.

As with many changes, when sponsorship is absent, awareness of the need for change and support for the change diminish as well.

Second, health care reform was labeled as the "Clinton" plan. Starr writes:

By putting his personal signature on health care re-
form, moreover, Clinton gave the Republicans an
incentive to defeat it and humiliate him rather than
compromise.

In the end, support also eroded on the part of small businesses' lobbies and health insurance companies. They did not just re-sist a particular element of health care reform; they resisted the change in general. An active television campaign directed at the American public cemented the death of this change.

In the context of the ADKAR model, this change failed from lack of desire, not from lack of knowledge. Starr concludes his article by stating that "the lesson for next time in health reform is faster, smaller."

In other words, your change cannot be larger than your sponsorship coalition can support, for it is that sponsorship co-alition and their activities that facilitate a desire to change. In the absence of desire, no amount of knowledge can produce change.

It is also possible that the policy reform team blurred awareness with desire. In the presence of very high awareness of the need for change, a common mistake is to assume that de-sire to support that change automatically follows. While it was evident that the American public was very aware that more and more people lacked health care coverage, support for wide-spread and dramatic reform in health care was sufficiently low to prevent passing of any new legislation.

From an educational perspective, the case study can be analyzed in segments. ADKAR allows a student of change management to make a clear delineation between knowledge and desire, and the nuances between awareness of a need for change and desire to support a change can be studied and discussed. As an educational framework, ADKAR focuses conversations toward the primary building blocks for successful change. Rather than have random classroom discussions that range from one end of the spectrum to another, each element of the ADKAR model can be addressed separately. When combined with the analysis of successful changes like the "Green" Hotels case study, students of change can learn the dynamics of the change process.

ADKAR to assist with organizational change management planning

Project teams that are applying change management will usually prepare plans for communications, sponsorship activities, training programs, coaching plans and other change management activities. The ADKAR model can be used as a checklist to evaluate the completeness and potential impact of these plans.

For example, assume that you have prepared a communications plan for your project. When complete, the communications plan should include your key messages, a schedule of events, the delivery mechanism for each event and the "sender" of the communication. If an ADKAR assessment of this plan were completed for the first element of the model, awareness, the questions would include:

- What elements in your communications plan include awareness-building programs or activities?

- Do your key messages for building awareness include why the change is happening, the risk of not changing, and the internal or external drivers that created the need for the change?

- How many times are these awareness messages reinforced throughout the entire communications plan?

- Is the awareness message sent by the primary sponsor?

- Is that awareness message reinforced by employees' direct supervisors?

- Are awareness messages sent only at the beginning of the project or do they continue during implementation?

- How will you gather feedback from employees to determine their level of awareness of the need for this change?

As the change management team works through all of their plans, ADKAR helps ensure that activities occur in the right sequence. For example, training should not preclude communications and sponsorship activities that build awareness and desire. If these activities are out of order, education programs fail because students are not yet ready to engage in the change.

To ensure that change management activities remain properly sequenced and aligned with employee readiness, checks can be performed at different stages of the process. For example, communications designed to produce *awareness* can be assessed for their effectiveness through employee feedback. Sponsorship activities designed to create *desire* can be assessed through supervisor interviews. Training programs designed to build *knowledge* can be assessed with training feedback and assessment tools during the training session. Figure 14-1 shows example feedback tools that could be used to determine progress toward each goal of the ADKAR model. This process enables a project team to gather feedback throughout the process and ensure that change management activities are having the results they were expecting.

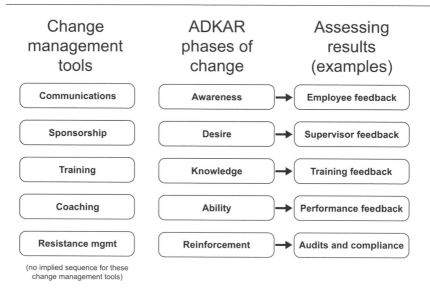

Change management tools	ADKAR phases of change	Assessing results (examples)
Communications	Awareness	→ Employee feedback
Sponsorship	Desire	→ Supervisor feedback
Training	Knowledge	→ Training feedback
Coaching	Ability	→ Performance feedback
Resistance mgmt	Reinforcement	→ Audits and compliance

(no implied sequence for these change management tools)

Figure 14-1 Assessing results of change management activities

I often encourage teams to use ADKAR like a litmus test. Apply the model to your completed plans and ask yourselves: Will our plans create the necessary building blocks for successful change? Through this process the team can refine and guide their change management work. Then collect feedback from employees and managers, and evaluate whether your change management activities accomplished their intended goals.

ADKAR as a coaching tool for managers and supervisors

Managers and supervisors can use ADKAR as a coaching tool with employees during change initiatives. Consider the many roles that supervisors already play with their employees, including:

- Communicator – the information channel for employees

- Problem-solver and coach – a place to go for help and direction

- Teacher and mentor – a source for knowledge and experience

- Advocate – a spokesperson for recognition and appreciation

Using the ADKAR model, managers and supervisors can use these same roles to manage change. For example, during the early phase of a change, managers are communicators. In this role, managers build *awareness* of the need for change and reinforce the messages sent by the executive sponsor, including why the change is happening, what the change means to the employee and the risk of not changing. Through one-on-one conversations, managers help employees translate the myriad of information about the change into meaningful terms.

As a change nears implementation, managers are problem solvers and coaches. In these roles they are instrumental in creating *desire* to support the change. They help employees sort out the impact of the change on a personal and professional level. Employees will have questions about "what's in it for me" and unresolved issues about how the change impacts their work. They may have personal barriers to the change that require assistance from their supervisor. In some cases employees may be resistant to the change. Supervisors are on the "front line" when managing resistance to a change. Managers in the role of coaches directly influence employees' desire to support and participate in the change.

During implementation, managers are teachers and mentors. Even with the best training programs, the on-the-job application of new tools, processes and job roles requires ongoing instruction and guidance. In this role managers are building *knowledge* on how to change. As employees engage in day-to-day work, gaps will become evident. Knowledge does not always translate to *ability* on the first try. Employees need an environment where they can practice and where it is safe to make mistakes. Managers are instrumental in creating a workplace where employees can develop new skills and abilities.

Finally, managers are advocates for their employees. Supervisors and managers play a key role in recognizing and rewarding the hard work and contributions of employees during the change process. These recognitions and rewards *reinforce* the change with employees so that the change is sustained in the organization.

Many effective managers play these roles every day. When managers are taught how to use ADKAR as a change management tool, they develop the competency to lead change.

ADKAR as an assessment tool for changes under way

For changes under way, ADKAR can be used to assess progress and to diagnose gaps in the change management program. Organization-wide ADKAR assessments help companies understand the barrier points and identify gaps. These assessments typically have two critical dimensions. First, the assessment allows employees to evaluate their position on each element of the ADKAR model. Second, employees are allowed to voice their current views within the assessment.

A sample assessment is shown in Figure 14-2. The structure of ADKAR assessments typically includes six question areas. The first question is about the change itself. The reason the assessment begins with a question about the change is because many employees have been misinformed about the nature of the change and how it will impact them. As a result of rumors and bad information, many of their perceptions are based on misunderstandings or partial information.

The remaining five questions follow the ADKAR model. These assessments can be completed with printed ADKAR worksheets or with web-based assessment tools. Additional information that is normally gathered with this assessment tool includes organization name, job type or level. In most cases the assessment is anonymous.

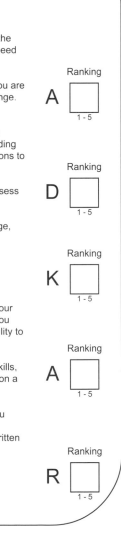

ADKAR® Assessment

Briefly describe the change that is being implemented at your workplace. Summarize the key elements of the change.

1. Describe your awareness of the need to change. What are the business, customer or competitor issues that have created a need to change? (written answers)

Review these reasons and ask yourself the degree to which you are aware of and understand all the business reasons for this change. Rank on a 1 to 5 scale (1 = lowest, 5 = highest).

A Ranking
1 - 5

2. List the motivating factors or consequences (good and bad) related to this change that impact your desire to change, including compelling reasons to support the change and specific objections to the change. (written answers)

Consider these motivating factors and potential objections. Assess your desire to change. Rank on a 1 to 5 scale.

D Ranking
1 - 5

3. List the skills and knowledge you need to support this change, both during and after the transition. (written answers)

Do you have a clear understanding of the required skills and knowledge? Have you received training or education in these areas? Rank on a 1 to 5 scale.

K Ranking
1 - 5

4. Considering the skills and knowledge from above, assess your overall ability to implement this change. What challenges do you foresee? What are the barriers inhibiting the organization's ability to realize this change? (written answers)

To what extent do you have the ability to implement the new skills, knowledge and behaviors associated with this change? Rank on a 1 to 5 scale.

A Ranking
1 - 5

5. List the reinforcements in your organization that will help you sustain the change. What incentives are in place to make the change stick? What incentives do not support the change? (written answers)

To what degree are reinforcements in place to support and maintain the change? Rank on a 1 to 5 scale.

R Ranking
1 - 5

Figure 14-2 ADKAR Assessment

Two results are extracted from the data of an ADKAR assessment:

- The barrier point to the change for the group overall

- Specific details that will help lead to resolution of key obstacles

For example, in a large assessment of a service agency undergoing major restructuring, the ADKAR assessment showed that 51% of the employees had moderate-to-low awareness of why the change was even needed. Nearly one-half of employees indicated moderate to low desire to support the change. The data was separated by functional groups, allowing the change management team to identify the barrier points for each group.

Second, specific information was extracted from the verbatim answers from employees. The data clearly identified specific areas where the change management process had broken down. Managers uncovered the missing pieces of information around awareness and they better understood the specific objections from employees. Armed with this new information, the primary sponsor and his leadership team were able to address these issues.

ADKAR assessment data can be segmented by function, location or level in the company. Different demographic slices can help the change management team identify the obstacles and focus energies in the right areas. Because not all groups move through change at the same rate, this type of group-by-group analysis provides critical steering for the change management team.

ADKAR as a planning tool for change

ADKAR can be used as a planning tool for individuals to promote ideas in presentations and meetings at work. For example, when preparing for a meeting or crafting an email in which you are putting a new idea forward, consider using the ADKAR model to structure the sequence of your material. Consider what elements would increase the awareness of the audience regarding the need for the change. Use this material first. Next consider what would be the pain points for this group. What would motivate them to embrace your idea and create a desire to change? Then consider what knowledge is required such that the group will know how to change. When addressing ability, anticipate potential barriers and address these proactively. Consider what actions you can take to reinforce the change. When ADKAR is used in this way to facilitate ideas or move an agenda forward, the results are faster adoption rates and greater acceptance of your work.

The ADKAR analysis worksheet provided next is an example of an exercise that a planning team can use to help guide their work.

ADKAR analysis worksheet

Purpose: to guide the development of the communication plan, sponsorship roadmap, coaching plan, training plan and resistance management plan.

Awareness

- Why is the change being made and what are the risks of not changing?

- What is the level of awareness of the need for this change today?

- Will building awareness be easy or difficult? Why?

Desire

- What are the motivating factors in support of this change (what would cause someone to support this change)?

- What are the opposing forces to this change (what would cause someone to object to this change)?

- Do you anticipate support or resistance to this change? Why?

Knowledge

- List the knowledge, skills and behaviors needed to support this change.

- Is the gap in knowledge, skills and behaviors large or small?

Ability

- Considering the skills and knowledge needed for this change, what potential challenges do you see for employees successfully implementing the change?

- What barriers may inhibit your organization from implementing this change?

Reinforcement

- What reinforcements would be necessary to sustain the change?

- What characteristics of the organization may cause the change not to be sustained?

Summary

The ADKAR model has five elements or objectives that must be achieved with individuals in order for change to be implemented and sustained. These elements form the basic building blocks for successful change:

1. **Awareness** of the need for change

2. **Desire** to support and participate in the change

3. **Knowledge** of how to change

4. **Ability** to implement the required skills and behaviors

5. **Reinforcement** to sustain the change

Once the ADKAR perspective is rooted into your process for analyzing change, you can readily apply it to any number of situations. You can develop a "new lens" through which to observe and influence change. You may be working for change in your public school system or in a small city council. You may be sponsoring change in your department at work. You may be observing large changes that are being attempted at the highest levels of government or you may be leading an enterprise-wide change initiative. The perspective enabled by the ADKAR model allows you to view change in a new way. You can begin to see the barrier points and understand the levers that can move your changes forward.

After 10 years of applying the ADKAR model with businesses, government agencies and local communities, I have observed the "light bulb" coming on time and time again. This simple model enables business managers to see change as a process.

The best phone call I ever received was from a business manager who was a former student in one of my classes. He started the call by saying, "I thought this model was too simple to be applicable."

I was unsure where the call was heading from that introductory remark, but before I could ask he went on to say, "But today I had an employee in my office who was struggling with one of our changes. This was a valued employee and I wanted to do the right thing, but found myself at a loss for what to say. I looked down at the small pencil box with the engraved ADKAR model, and thought, why not, let's give it a try."

He paused for a moment, leaving me somewhat anxious for the outcome of his meeting. Rather than tell me the details, he simply said, "That's why I called. Just to say thank you. It worked. I just wanted to let you know."

References

Chapter 2

1. NRET Theme Papers on Implementing Codes of Practice in the Fresh Produce Industry, http://www.nri.org/NRET/overview.htm, 2002.

2. *Best Practices in Change Management* report, Prosci, 2005.

3. Keys, C. *Creating an Awareness of Hazards: Some NSW Examples relating to Floods and Storms*, paper presented to the Conference on Atmospheric Hazards: Process, Awareness and Response, University of Queensland, Brisbane, 1995.

4. Kastelic, J. and Posch, K. *Marketing Park Pricing Incentives for Low Emission Vehicles*, presented at European Conference on Mobility Management, 2004.

5. *Dell Sees Green In EPA Computer, Recycling Pact*, http://news.com.com/Dell+sees+green+in+EPA+computer,+recycling+pact/2100-1003_3-5179278.html, 2004.

6. Kirton, M.J. *Adaption-Innovation*, Psychology Press, 2003.

7. Best Practices in Change Management report, Prosci, 2003.

Chapter 3

1. Author's note: The expectation that a person has that they will be successful with a change, combined with his or her unique intrinsic motivators, is referred to as Expectancy Theory. More information can be found in Victor H. Vroom's book titled Work and Motivation, Jossey-Bass Publishers, 1995.

Chapter 6

1. *Motivating Call Center Agents,* Call Center Learning Center, Prosci, 2004.

Chapter 7

1. Bartlett, R. *Our Dependence on Oil*, http://www.energybulletin.net/5519.html, 2005.

2. *Set America Free: Cut dependence on foreign oil,* http://www.setamericafree.org/openletter.htm

3. Author's note: Remarks by Chairman Alan Greenspan before the Japan Business Federation, the Japan Chamber of Commerce and Industry, and the Japan Association of Corporate Executives, Tokyo, Japan, October 17, 2005, http://www.federalreserve.gov/BoardDocs/Speeches/2005/20051017/default.htm

Chapter 8

1. Author's note: Prosci is the sponsor of the Change Management Learning Center. More information on this study of sponsor roles can be found at www.change-management.com or in the 2005 report, Best Practices in Change Management.

2. *Best Practices in Change Management* report, Prosci, 2005.

Chapter 9

1. Goleman, D. et al. *Primal Leadership: Learning to Lead with Emotional Intelligence,* Harvard Business School Press, 2004.

2. *Best Practices in Change Management* report (411 participating organizations), Prosci, 2005.

3. Johnson, S. *Who Moved My Cheese?,* Putnam, 1998.

4. *Best Practices in Change Management* report, Prosci, 2005.

Chapter 10

1. Knowles, Malcolm S. *The Modern Practice of Adult Education,* Prentice Hall/Cambridge, 1980.

2. Pike, Robert W. *Creative Training Techniques Handbook,* HRD Press, 2003.

3. Merriam, Sharan B. and Caffarella, Rosemary S. *Learning in Adulthood,* Jossey-Bass Publishers, 1999.

Chapter 14

1. *What Happened to Health Care Reform?,* http://www.princeton.edu/~starr/20starr.html

Jeff Hiatt is the president of Prosci Research and founder of the Change Management Learning Center. He is the author of the book Employee's Survival Guide to Change and co-author of Change Management: the people side of change. Jeff was a Distinguished Member of the Technical Staff at Bell Laboratories from 1985 to 1995 where he co-authored Winning with Quality, a story of business and quality improvement for one of AT&T's product divisions. After founding Prosci in 1996, he has led research in change management with more than 900 companies from 59 countries. He is also a frequent guest speaker for executive leadership teams and conferences.